The Upgrade Code   Joshua J. Bowen

Table of Contents

Forward

This book is a culmination of my journey—a journey of discovery, transformation, and growth. It was born from a deep desire to understand the mechanisms of the mind and the invisible forces that shape our lives. Over time, the teachings of great thought leaders and the timeless concepts they explored helped me reframe my understanding of myself and the world. Through their wisdom, I learned that the code of our inner software—our beliefs, habits, and perceptions—can be rewritten to unlock our fullest potential. *The Upgrade Code* is my way of sharing these life-changing principles with you, in the hope that they inspire and empower you as profoundly as they have me.

Introduction: Rewriting the Code of Your Mind

I magine your mind as a powerful computer, capable of extraordinary calculations, creativity, and problem-solving. Yet, like any computer, it runs on software—programs written over time by your environment, experiences, and beliefs. Some of this code is outdated, riddled with bugs, and no longer serves you. What if you could rewrite it? What if you could install new programs to help you master your health, wealth, relationships, and personal growth?

This book is about doing just that.

Throughout history, great thinkers like Joseph Murphy, Émile Coué, Napoleon Hill, and modern teachers of *The Secret* have uncovered timeless principles about the power of the mind and the nature of reality. Each offered tools to transform your thoughts, align your emotions, and create a life you love. This book combines their wisdom into a modern system called *The Upgrade Code*—a step-by-step guide to rewiring your mind, aligning your energy, and taking inspired action.

The Upgrade Code isn't magic—it's a process. It's not just about thinking positively; it's about learning how to direct the immense power of your subconscious mind, harmonize with the universe, and take meaningful steps toward your dreams. By the end of this book, you'll have the tools to rewrite your inner software, upgrade your reality, and master your life.

Are you ready to install the code?

Part 1: The Foundation of Your Software

Overview of Chapter 1: The Subconscious as Your Operating System

Your subconscious mind is the silent powerhouse behind every decision, habit, and outcome in your life. Joseph Murphy called it "the infinite intelligence within you." It's the part of your mind that never sleeps, never takes a break, and constantly works to make your life match the patterns it has been programmed with.

How the Subconscious Works

Think of your mind as an iceberg. The conscious mind—the part you use to analyze, plan, and make decisions—is just the tip of the iceberg. Below the surface lies the vast subconscious, which controls 95% of your behavior. It's responsible for your automatic thoughts, emotions, and habits.

When your subconscious is programmed with empowering beliefs, you naturally take actions that lead to success. But if it's filled with limiting beliefs —like "I'm not good enough" or "I'll never be wealthy"—it sabotages you, no matter how hard you consciously try to succeed.

Your Mind as Software

Let's extend the iceberg analogy with something more modern: your mind as a computer. Your conscious mind is the keyboard and mouse—it inputs commands. Your subconscious is the operating system that runs in the background. If the operating system is outdated or corrupted, the computer won't function properly, no matter how good the user is.

The good news? You can reprogram your subconscious. Just like software, it can be upgraded with new beliefs, patterns, and habits.

Chapter 1: The Subconscious as Your Operating System

Your subconscious mind is the unseen powerhouse behind every thought, decision, and action you take. It's the silent driver of your life, influencing everything from your habits to your emotions, relationships, and success. But like any operating system, its effectiveness depends on the code it runs. In this chapter, we'll dive deeper into understanding your subconscious and how you can harness its immense power to transform your life.

Imagine this: You're sitting at your computer, and it suddenly freezes. No matter how much you click or type, nothing responds. Frustration builds, and you realize the issue isn't with the programs you're running—it's buried deep in the operating system. Now, think of your mind as that computer. Beneath your conscious decisions and actions lies your subconscious—the operating system driving every thought, belief, and habit. If its programming is outdated or corrupted, it can silently sabotage your efforts, no matter how determined you are. The good news? You can rewrite the code.

What is the Subconscious Mind?

The subconscious mind is the part of your mental system that operates below your conscious awareness. It manages automatic processes—like your heartbeat and breathing—but it also stores your beliefs, emotions, memories, and habits. These internalized programs influence your behavior and outcomes, often without you realizing it.

Take Anna, for example. Growing up, Anna's parents frequently told her, "Money doesn't grow on trees." As an adult, no matter how much she earned, she found herself living paycheck to paycheck. Her subconscious mind had absorbed the belief that money was scarce and hard to come by. Until Anna consciously rewrote this belief, her actions and decisions continued to align with a scarcity mindset, holding her back from financial abundance.

Key Characteristics of the Subconscious Mind

- **Autonomous Operation:** The subconscious runs on autopilot. Once a habit or belief is embedded, it repeats the pattern without conscious effort.

- **Emotional Storage:** It holds emotional memories, especially from impactful experiences, which shape how you view yourself and the world.

- **Literal Nature:** The subconscious takes everything at face value. It doesn't analyze or question—it simply accepts repeated inputs as truth.

- **Connection to the Body:** It influences physical responses like stress, relaxation, and even healing. Your body reacts to subconscious thoughts as if they are real.

How Does the Subconscious Affect Your Life?

Think of your subconscious as a GPS. When programmed correctly, it guides you effortlessly toward your destination. But if it's running faulty or outdated instructions, it can lead you astray. For example:

- A subconscious belief like "I'm not good enough" may cause you to avoid opportunities, even when they're within reach.

- Positive programming like "I always find solutions" enables you to face challenges with confidence.

Consider Eric, a talented artist who struggled to promote his work. Beneath his conscious desire for success was a subconscious belief: "Artists can't make a living." This belief sabotaged his efforts until he learned to reprogram it with empowering affirmations and visualization techniques. Once he rewrote the belief to "My art brings value and abundance," opportunities began to flow.

Your subconscious also filters information through a mechanism called the Reticular Activating System (RAS). The RAS acts as a gatekeeper, highlighting information that aligns with your subconscious programming. If you believe "the world is full of opportunities," your RAS will help you notice them. If you believe "nothing ever works out for me," your RAS will focus on confirming that belief.

The Subconscious and Neuroplasticity

The exciting truth is that your subconscious is not fixed. Thanks to neuroplasticity—the brain's ability to rewire itself—you can update old programming with new beliefs and habits. This rewiring process occurs through:

- **Repetition:** Repeated thoughts and behaviors create stronger neural pathways.

- **Emotion:** Emotionally charged experiences leave a lasting impression on the subconscious.

- **Visualization:** Mental rehearsal activates the same neural circuits as real-life experiences, helping to embed new patterns.

Think of your subconscious as a garden. Each thought you plant is a seed. Repetition and emotion are the sunlight and water that help it grow. If you consistently plant seeds of doubt or fear, those weeds will take over. But if you plant seeds of confidence, abundance, and joy, your garden will flourish.

Signs Your Subconscious Needs an Upgrade

If you've ever felt stuck despite your best efforts, it's likely due to conflicting subconscious programming. Here are some signs that your subconscious is working against you:

- **Procrastination:** You know what you need to do but avoid taking action.

- **Negative Self-Talk:** Persistent thoughts like "I can't" or "I'll fail" dominate your inner dialogue.

- **Self-Sabotage:** You start making progress, only to undo your efforts.

- **Repeating Patterns:** The same challenges show up in your finances, relationships, or health.

- **Fear of Success:** Achieving your goals feels overwhelming or "too good to be true."

Understanding Subconscious Programming

Your subconscious mind was programmed primarily during childhood, when your brain was most impressionable. Early experiences, repeated messages, and emotional events shaped your core beliefs. For example:

- If your parents often said, "We can't afford that," you might have absorbed a scarcity mindset around money.

- If you were praised for academic achievements, you might have developed a belief that success equals self-worth.

These programs become the default settings for your life, influencing your decisions and outcomes until you consciously choose to change them.

How to Access and Influence the Subconscious

Changing your subconscious programming requires a combination of awareness and intentional practice. Here are the key tools to access and reprogram it:

- **Meditation:**

  - Meditation quiets the conscious mind, making it easier to access the subconscious.

  - *Simple Practice:* Sit quietly for 5–10 minutes, focus on your breath, and allow thoughts to flow without judgment.

- **Affirmations:**

  - Affirmations are positive, present-tense statements that replace negative beliefs.

  - *Example:* Replace "I'm not good enough" with "I am worthy and capable."

- **Visualization:**

  o Create vivid mental images of your desired outcomes. The subconscious responds powerfully to imagery combined with emotion.

- **Autosuggestion:**

  o Repeatedly suggest new ideas to yourself through written or spoken affirmations.

  o *Example:* Write "I am successful" 10 times every morning.

- **Journaling:**

  o Reflect on limiting beliefs and consciously rewrite them.

  o *Prompt:* "What belief is holding me back? What belief do I want to replace it with?"

- **Emotional Anchoring:**

- Attach positive emotions to your new beliefs through gratitude or excitement.

- *Example:* Feel genuine joy as you visualize achieving your goal.

Practical Exercise: Reprogramming Your Subconscious

1. **Identify a Limiting Belief**

   - Choose one area of your life where you feel stuck. Write down the belief or thought that arises when you think about this area.

   - *Example:* "I'm not smart enough to start my own business."

2. **Create a New Belief**

   - Write a positive affirmation that directly counters the limiting belief.

   - *Example:* "I am intelligent, resourceful, and capable of achieving my goals."

3. **Reinforce the New Belief**

  o   Practice the following daily for 21 days:

  - Repeat your affirmation aloud 10 times in the morning and evening.

  - Visualize yourself embodying the new belief in specific scenarios.

  - Write your affirmation in a journal each day.

The Power of Rewriting Your Subconscious

Reprogramming your subconscious mind is like updating your operating system. It may take time and consistent effort, but the results are transformative. By aligning your subconscious with your conscious goals, you'll find that actions flow more naturally, opportunities appear more frequently, and success feels more attainable.

In the next chapter, we'll explore one of the most effective tools for subconscious reprogramming: autosuggestion. This simple yet powerful technique can accelerate your journey toward mastering your mind and your life.

Overview of Chapter 2: Autosuggestion: Writing Your Code

One of the simplest yet most powerful tools to reprogram your subconscious is autosuggestion. Émile Coué, the father of this technique, discovered that when people repeat positive affirmations with emotion and belief, their subconscious accepts these suggestions as truth.

Why Autosuggestion Works

The subconscious doesn't distinguish between real and imagined experiences. When you visualize success, repeat affirmations, or imagine your ideal life, your subconscious treats these inputs as real and adjusts your thoughts and actions accordingly.

The Power of Repetition

Coué's famous affirmation, *"Every day, in every way, I am getting better and better,"* encapsulates the principle of autosuggestion. By repeating this phrase with conviction, countless people have transformed their health, confidence, and circumstances. Repetition is key—each repetition reinforces the new "code" in your subconscious.

How to Use Autosuggestion

Here's a simple formula for creating and using affirmations:

1. **Be Specific**: Focus on a clear goal. For example, instead of saying, "I want to be wealthy," say, "I am attracting $10,000 in new opportunities this month."
2. **Use the Present Tense**: Speak as if it's already true. Your subconscious responds to certainty, not wishful thinking.
3. **Feel the Emotion**: Emotion is the fuel for autosuggestion. Imagine the joy, excitement, or gratitude of achieving your goal as you repeat your affirmation.
4. **Repetition**: Repeat your affirmation daily— morning and night—for 21 days to create a lasting shift.

Chapter 2: Autosuggestion: Writing Your Code

I magine waking up every morning with a nagging voice in your head whispering, "You're not good enough." Now imagine that same voice being replaced by one that says, "You're capable of extraordinary things." Which voice would set the tone for your day? This is the transformative power of autosuggestion—a tool that lets you intentionally write the code for your subconscious mind, shaping the narrative that guides your life.

Autosuggestion, the process of feeding your subconscious mind positive and empowering statements, isn't just wishful thinking. It's a scientifically backed technique that has been used for centuries to reprogram beliefs, shift mindsets, and achieve success. In this chapter, we'll explore what autosuggestion is, why it works, and how you can harness it to create profound changes in your life.

What is Autosuggestion?

At its core, autosuggestion is the practice of repeating positive, present-tense affirmations to influence your subconscious mind. Coined by French psychologist Émile Coué in the early 20th century, autosuggestion is grounded in the idea that the subconscious mind accepts repeated statements as truth. These statements, when infused with emotion and belief, become the new programming for your subconscious operating system.

The Origins of Autosuggestion

Coué's work revolutionized how people viewed the mind's potential. His famous affirmation, "Every day, in every way, I am getting better and better," became a cornerstone of his method. Coué believed that consistent repetition of positive statements could override negative thought patterns and lead to physical, emotional, and mental transformation. His work was ahead of its time, blending psychological insight with practical application in a way that remains relevant today.

How Autosuggestion Shapes Reality

The subconscious mind doesn't differentiate between fact and fiction; it accepts whatever it's repeatedly told. This is why autosuggestion has the power to reshape reality. Think of your subconscious as a fertile garden. Whatever seeds you plant—whether positive or negative—will grow. Autosuggestion is the deliberate planting of seeds that align with your goals and aspirations.

Take Sarah, for example. After years of believing she wasn't smart enough to advance in her career, she discovered autosuggestion. Every morning and evening, she repeated the affirmation, "I am intelligent, resourceful, and capable of achieving my goals." At first, it felt awkward, even untrue. But over time, her subconscious began to internalize this message. Within months, Sarah found herself taking on challenges she once avoided, impressing her colleagues, and earning a promotion she had only dreamed of.

Autosuggestion vs. Wishful Thinking

It's important to distinguish autosuggestion from mere wishful thinking. Autosuggestion is an active, intentional process that combines repetition, belief, and emotion. While wishful thinking lacks structure and commitment, autosuggestion requires consistent effort to rewire deeply ingrained beliefs. The difference lies in action—autosuggestion encourages alignment between thoughts and behaviors, creating a pathway for real change.

Why Does Autosuggestion Work?

The subconscious mind is impressionable. It doesn't distinguish between truth and fiction; it simply absorbs repeated inputs as reality. This is why autosuggestion can have such a profound impact on your thoughts, behaviors, and outcomes.

The Science Behind Autosuggestion

Research on neuroplasticity shows that repeated thoughts strengthen neural pathways in the brain. Autosuggestion works by:

- **Creating New Neural Connections:** Repetition rewires the brain, replacing old, limiting beliefs with new, empowering ones.

- **Engaging the Reticular Activating System (RAS):** Your RAS filters information based on your subconscious programming. Positive affirmations direct your RAS to notice opportunities and solutions that align with your goals.

- **Triggering the Emotional Brain:** Emotion amplifies the impact of affirmations, embedding them deeper into the subconscious.

Consider athletes who use mental rehearsal—a form of autosuggestion—to improve performance. Studies have shown that vividly imagining success activates the same neural circuits as physically practicing a skill. The brain accepts the imagined scenario as real, preparing the body and mind for achievement.

Emotional Amplification

The effectiveness of autosuggestion is greatly enhanced by emotion. Simply repeating words without feeling their significance reduces their impact. For example, saying, "I am confident" while imagining a moment of pride and achievement creates a powerful emotional anchor. This emotional reinforcement accelerates the process of embedding new beliefs into the subconscious.

How to Craft Effective Autosuggestions

Not all affirmations are created equal. To maximize the power of autosuggestion, your affirmations should be:

- **Positive:** Focus on what you want, not what you're trying to avoid.

    - Ineffective: "I'm not bad at managing money."

- ○ Effective: "I manage my money with ease and confidence."

- **Present-Tense:** Speak as if the desired outcome is already true. This creates a sense of certainty that your subconscious responds to.

  - ○ Example: "I am healthy and energized every day."

- **Specific and Personal:** Tailor affirmations to your unique goals and values.

  - ○ Example: "I attract clients who value my creativity and expertise."

- **Emotional:** Infuse your affirmations with excitement, gratitude, or joy. Emotion is the catalyst that drives change.

Practical Steps to Use Autosuggestion

1. **Identify Your Limiting Beliefs:**

   ○ Reflect on areas of your life where you feel stuck. What beliefs might be holding you back?

   ○ Example: "I'm not confident enough to speak in public."

2. **Create a New Affirmation:**

   ○ Write a positive, empowering statement that counters the limiting belief.

   ○ Example: "I speak with clarity, confidence, and ease in every situation."

3. **Repeat Your Affirmation Daily:**

   ○ Set aside time each morning and evening to repeat your affirmations aloud or silently. Aim for at least 5–10 minutes.

- o   Pro Tip: Use a mirror to amplify the connection and confidence in your affirmations.

4. **Visualize Your Success:**

   - o   Pair your affirmations with vivid mental imagery of achieving your goal. Imagine how it feels, looks, and sounds.

5. **Anchor Your Affirmation with Emotion:**

   - o   As you repeat your affirmations, feel the emotions associated with success. Gratitude, excitement, and joy make your affirmations more impactful.

6. **Write It Down:**

   - o   Keep a journal to record your affirmations and reflect on progress. Writing reinforces the message in your subconscious.

Real-Life Stories of Transformation

John had spent years doubting his ability to lead. When he was promoted to a management role, his fear of failure was overwhelming. He couldn't shake the feeling that he wasn't cut out for leadership and would soon be exposed as inadequate. Every meeting felt like an ordeal, and every decision seemed to confirm his fears. Desperate for change, John confided in a mentor who introduced him to autosuggestion.

John began with a simple affirmation: "I am a confident and effective leader who inspires my team." Each morning, he repeated it aloud while looking in the mirror, imagining himself leading with authority and compassion. At night, he visualized his team's faces, their engagement, and their gratitude for his guidance. Slowly, something shifted. Within weeks, his tone of voice grew steadier, his decision-making more assured. His team noticed and responded — meetings became collaborative, and performance improved. By the end of the quarter, John had not only met his goals but exceeded them, finally recognizing himself as the capable leader he always aspired to be.

Maya's story is equally inspiring. As an aspiring entrepreneur, Maya had always dreamed of starting her own business but felt paralyzed by impostor syndrome. The voice in her head constantly whispered, "Who are you to think you can succeed?" For years, this internal dialogue held her back. Then, she discovered autosuggestion. Her affirmation became her lifeline: "I am a visionary business owner who creates value and opportunity."

Every day, Maya would repeat this mantra while journaling about the kind of business she wanted to create. She visualized her customers delighted by her products, her business thriving, and her team celebrating milestones. With each repetition, her belief in herself grew. When the opportunity to pitch her idea to investors arose, she took the leap. Her pitch was met with enthusiasm, and she secured the funding to launch her startup. Today, Maya's business is thriving, a testament to the power of rewriting one's inner script.

Common Challenges and How to Overcome Them

- **Doubt or Skepticism:** If affirmations feel untrue, start small. Use bridge statements like, "I am learning to..." or "I am open to..." to ease into new beliefs.

- **Inconsistency:** Set a routine. Attach your autosuggestion practice to an existing habit, like brushing your teeth.

- **Impatience:** Remember, change takes time. Commit to 21 days of consistent practice to create lasting shifts.

Practical Exercise: Your Daily Affirmation Ritual

1. Write down one area of your life where you want change.

     - Example: Career advancement.

2. Craft an affirmation that reflects your desired outcome.

     - Example: "I am thriving in a fulfilling career that aligns with my passions and talents."

3. Spend 5 minutes each morning repeating your affirmation aloud.

4. Visualize your desired outcome while repeating your affirmation. Feel the emotions of success as if it's already real.

5. Journal your experiences and any progress you notice over time.

The Power of Autosuggestion

Autosuggestion isn't about pretending problems don't exist. It's about rewiring your mind to approach challenges with resilience, confidence, and clarity. By intentionally feeding your subconscious empowering messages, you become the author of your story rather than a passive character in someone else's narrative.

In the next chapter, we'll explore visualization—a technique that takes the principles of autosuggestion and amplifies them with the power of imagination. Get ready to see your goals come to life in vivid detail and learn how to turn dreams into reality.

Common Mistakes to Avoid

- **Lack of Consistency**: Sporadic practice weakens the impact.
- **Negativity in Language**: Avoid phrases like "I will stop being bad at this." Focus on what you want to achieve instead.
- **Lack of Emotion**: Affirmations without feeling are less effective.

Overview of Chapter 3: Faith, Imagination, and Visualization

Napoleon Hill famously said, "Whatever the mind can conceive and believe, it can achieve." Faith and imagination are two of the most powerful tools for shaping your subconscious mind and manifesting your desires.

Faith: The Foundation of Belief

Faith is more than just hoping something will happen; it's the unwavering belief that it will. When you believe in your ability to succeed, you align your thoughts and actions with that belief. Hill argued that faith is a state of mind that can be cultivated through affirmation, visualization, and persistence.

Imagination: The Blueprint of Reality

Your imagination is the creative workshop of your mind. When you visualize your goals as already achieved, you create a mental blueprint for the subconscious to follow. Visualization connects your emotions with your desires, making them feel real.

The Science of Visualization

Research shows that the brain doesn't differentiate between vividly imagined experiences and real ones. Athletes, for example, use mental rehearsal to improve performance. By visualizing success, you prime your brain to recognize opportunities and take actions that lead to that outcome.

Chapter 3: Faith, Imagination, and Visualization: Bridging Desires to Reality

I magine standing on one side of a canyon, staring across at your dream life on the other side. The gap seems vast and unbridgeable. Yet, within you lies the power to cross it—the twin forces of faith and imagination. These tools, when wielded effectively, become the bridge between your desires and reality. Napoleon Hill, in *Think and Grow Rich*, taught that faith is not merely a fleeting feeling but a cultivated state of mind. Combined with imagination, it allows you to visualize a world of possibilities far beyond your current circumstances.

This chapter delves into how faith and imagination work together to unlock the potential of your subconscious, providing the clarity and conviction needed to pursue your goals.

The Role of Faith: A Foundation of Belief

Faith is more than hope; it's a deep, unshakable belief in your ability to achieve your goals. It's the mental glue that holds your vision together, especially when faced with challenges. Faith aligns your thoughts, emotions, and actions, transforming abstract desires into tangible outcomes.

Faith as a Catalyst for Change

Faith operates by:

- **Replacing Fear with Confidence:** Fear and doubt often cloud our ability to take meaningful action. Faith clears the fog, providing the clarity needed to move forward.

- **Activating the Subconscious Mind:** When you believe deeply in a goal, your subconscious begins to work tirelessly to find solutions and opportunities to achieve it.

- **Strengthening Resilience:** Faith fuels persistence. Even in the face of setbacks, it keeps you moving, reminding you that challenges are temporary.

Consider Mark, who once doubted his ability to run a marathon. Every time he began training, the thought, "I'm not a runner," sabotaged his progress. But when a friend introduced him to faith-building techniques, Mark began repeating affirmations: "I am strong, determined, and capable of finishing a marathon." Over time, this belief replaced his doubts. With consistent training and unwavering faith in his ability, Mark crossed the finish line, accomplishing what once seemed impossible.

How to Cultivate Faith

1. **Reframe Your Beliefs:** Identify limiting beliefs and actively replace them with empowering ones. For example, shift "I'm not good at this" to "I am learning and growing every day."

2. **Immerse Yourself in Positivity:** Surround yourself with people, books, and environments that reinforce your belief in your goals.

3. **Take Consistent Action:** Faith grows with evidence. Every small step toward your goal strengthens your belief in its achievability.

4. **Practice Gratitude:** Gratitude shifts focus from what you lack to what you have, creating a mindset of abundance and possibility.

Imagination: Your Creative Workshop

Imagination is the playground where dreams take form. It allows you to visualize possibilities beyond your current reality, acting as a rehearsal for your desired future. Through imagination, you construct vivid mental blueprints that guide your subconscious toward your goals.

How Imagination Transforms Desires

Imagination brings abstract desires into vivid focus. It connects emotions to goals, making them feel real and within reach. For instance, envisioning the joy of receiving a long-awaited job offer ignites the motivation needed to prepare for interviews and network effectively.

The Science of Visualization

Research has shown that visualization activates the same neural circuits as real-life experiences. When you vividly imagine achieving a goal, your brain interprets it as already happening. This strengthens your belief in its attainability and primes your mind to recognize and seize opportunities.

Neural Activation and Rewiring

Visualization works by leveraging the brain's neuroplasticity — its ability to rewire itself based on repeated experiences. When you vividly imagine a scenario, your brain creates or strengthens neural pathways associated with that experience. These pathways act as mental shortcuts, enabling you to respond more effectively when opportunities arise. For instance, if you visualize yourself confidently giving a speech, your brain rehearses the actions and emotions involved, making the actual event feel familiar and achievable.

Athletic Performance and Visualization

Athletes frequently use visualization to enhance performance. Olympic swimmers, for example, mentally rehearse their races in meticulous detail, imagining every stroke, turn, and finish. This practice does more than boost confidence; it prepares the brain and body for success. Studies have shown that athletes who combine physical practice with visualization perform better than those who rely solely on physical training.

One famous example comes from basketball. Researchers conducted a study where players were divided into three groups: one practiced free throws physically, another visualized making successful free throws, and the third did nothing. Remarkably, the group that visualized performed almost as well as the group that practiced physically. This demonstrates how powerful visualization can be in reinforcing skills and improving outcomes.

Everyday Applications of Visualization

While visualization is widely associated with sports, its benefits extend far beyond the athletic field. Consider a professional preparing for a job interview. By visualizing the interview process—walking into the room, confidently answering questions, and receiving positive feedback—they not only reduce anxiety but also increase their likelihood of success. The brain, having rehearsed the scenario, perceives it as familiar and less intimidating.

Visualization can also be a powerful tool for personal development. Imagine someone aiming to improve their financial situation. By vividly picturing themselves budgeting wisely, receiving a promotion, or paying off debts, they prime their subconscious to recognize and act on opportunities aligned with these goals.

The Role of Emotion in Visualization

Visualization is most effective when paired with strong emotions. Simply imagining a scenario is not enough; you must feel the joy, excitement, and satisfaction of achieving your goal. These emotions serve as a signal to your subconscious, reinforcing the belief that your goal is both desirable and attainable. For example, when visualizing a successful career, imagine not only the accolades but also the pride and gratitude that come with them.

Emotional engagement amplifies the brain's response to visualization. Studies have shown that when individuals visualize scenarios with intense emotions, their brains release dopamine—a chemical associated with motivation and reward. This creates a positive feedback loop, encouraging repeated visualization and action toward the goal.

How to Practice Visualization

Visualization is a skill that grows stronger with practice. Here's a step-by-step guide to making it a daily habit:

1. **Define Your Goal:**

    - Be clear and specific about what you want to achieve.

    - Example: "I want to earn $10,000 per month doing work I love."

2. **Create a Mental Movie:**

    - Close your eyes and imagine yourself living your goal. Picture the environment, people, and events involved.

    - Example: Visualize receiving a paycheck, celebrating with loved ones, and feeling immense gratitude.

3. **Engage All Senses:**

    ○   Add vivid details—what do you see, hear, feel, smell, and taste?

    ○   Example: Hear the applause as you give a successful presentation or feel the crisp paper of a check in your hands.

4. **Anchor Positive Emotions:**

    ○   Feel the joy, excitement, and satisfaction of achieving your goal as if it's already happened. Emotions amplify the impact of visualization.

5. **Practice Daily:**

    ○   Spend 5–10 minutes visualizing your goal each morning or night. Consistency is key to embedding this vision into your subconscious.

Real-Life Stories of Faith and Imagination

Faith and imagination have transformed countless lives. Like Ella, a struggling artist who dreamed of having her work featured in galleries. For years, self-doubt held her back. One day, she decided to combine faith with visualization. Each night, she imagined her paintings hanging in prestigious galleries, crowds admiring her work, and buyers eagerly bidding.

Ella's visualization sessions were infused with gratitude and excitement. Over time, she noticed a shift. She began networking confidently, sharing her portfolio, and seizing opportunities. Within a year, Ella's art was showcased in multiple galleries, validating the power of her imagination.

Similarly, David, an entrepreneur, relied on faith to navigate a challenging business downturn. He adopted the mantra, "I am resilient and capable of turning challenges into opportunities." Through daily visualization, he imagined his company thriving—seeing bustling offices, satisfied clients, and rising profits. Fueled by unwavering faith and a clear mental picture, David pivoted his business strategy, leading it to not only survive but thrive in a competitive market.

Overcoming Challenges in Faith and Visualization

While faith and imagination are powerful, they can be met with internal resistance. Here's how to address common obstacles:

- **Doubt:** Begin with small, believable steps. Build faith gradually by focusing on minor achievements.

- **Negative Imagery:** If negative thoughts intrude, consciously replace them with positive images. Redirect your focus to what you want, not what you fear.

- **Impatience:** Trust the process. Remember that change takes time and consistency.

Practical Exercise: Building Your Faith and Imagination Ritual

1. Write down one major goal you want to achieve.

2. Create an affirmation that reflects unwavering belief in this goal.

   ◦ Example: "I am a successful writer whose work inspires thousands."

3. Spend 5 minutes each morning visualizing your goal as achieved. Engage all senses and emotions.

4. Journal any progress, opportunities, or insights that arise as you practice this ritual.

The Power of Faith and Imagination

Faith and imagination are the dynamic duo that unlock the potential of your subconscious mind. Faith provides the conviction to act, while imagination paints the vision of what's possible. Together, they create a powerful synergy that propels you toward your goals.

As you continue your journey, remember that these tools are not reserved for the extraordinary—they are accessible to everyone. With consistent practice, you can cultivate faith, harness imagination, and build the bridge to the life you've always desired.

In the next chapter, we'll dive into the principles of the Law of Attraction and learn how to align your energy with your desires to manifest your dreams.

Practical Visualization Exercise

1. Close your eyes and take a few deep breaths.
2. Imagine your goal as already achieved. What does it look like? Feel like? Sound like?
3. Engage all your senses. Make the scene as vivid and detailed as possible.
4. Spend 5–10 minutes daily visualizing your success.

Practical Exercise: Vision Board Creation

Step 1: Gather images, quotes, and symbols that represent your goals.

Step 2: Arrange them on a board where you can see them daily.

Step 3: Spend a few minutes each day focusing on your vision board, imagining each element as part of your reality.

Overview of Chapter 4: The Law of Attraction: Setting Your Frequency

The Law of Attraction, popularized by *The Secret*, is rooted in the idea that "like attracts like." Your thoughts and emotions emit a vibrational frequency that influences the reality you experience. Simply put, the energy you project into the universe determines what you attract into your life.

Understanding Vibrations and Energy

Everything in the universe, including your thoughts, is made of energy. When you focus on positive thoughts and feelings, you raise your vibrational frequency, aligning yourself with desirable outcomes. Conversely, negative thoughts lower your vibration, attracting obstacles and challenges.

The Role of Focus

The Law of Attraction operates through your dominant focus. If you constantly worry about debt, for instance, you inadvertently attract more debt. Shifting your focus to abundance, gratitude, and opportunities changes your frequency and aligns you with wealth.

Practical Application: Setting Your Frequency

1. **Awareness**: Begin by observing your dominant thoughts and emotions. Are they aligned with your goals, or do they reflect fear and doubt?

2. **Shift Your Focus**: When negative thoughts arise, consciously redirect your focus to positive outcomes. Use affirmations and gratitude practices to reinforce this shift.

3. **Feel It Now**: Act as if you've already achieved your goal. Emotions like joy, gratitude, and excitement amplify your frequency.

Chapter 4: The Law of Attraction: Setting Your Frequency

I magine you are a radio tower, constantly transmitting and receiving signals. The thoughts you think, the emotions you feel, and the beliefs you hold determine the frequency you broadcast to the world. This is the essence of the Law of Attraction, a universal principle popularized by Rhonda Byrne in her groundbreaking work, *The Secret*. Byrne brought the concept into the mainstream, explaining that the energy you project into the universe determines the experiences you attract. Simply put, "like attracts like."

The Law of Attraction is not a new idea. Philosophers, spiritual teachers, and scientists have long discussed its principles. Wallace Wattles, in his classic *The Science of Getting Rich*, emphasized the importance of focused thought, stating, "By thought, the thing you want is brought to you; by action, you receive it." Similarly, Bob Proctor, one of the thinkers featured in *The Secret*, explained, "Thoughts become things. If you see it in your mind, you can hold it in your hand." These insights reveal a profound truth: your thoughts and emotions are powerful forces that shape your reality.

Imagine this: every thought you think sends out a signal, like tuning into a radio station. Positive, high-frequency thoughts broadcast joy, abundance, and love, attracting similar experiences. Negative, low-frequency thoughts, however, transmit fear, doubt, and lack, inviting obstacles and challenges. As Lisa Nichols, another prominent speaker in *The Secret*, said, "Your entire life is a reflection of how you think."

This universal principle transcends cultures and eras. Ancient texts like the *Upanishads* and *The Emerald Tablet* hinted at similar concepts, emphasizing the power of thought and intention in shaping reality. Modern psychology, too, underscores the impact of mindset on outcomes. As Dr. Joe Dispenza explained, "When you think from your future, instead of your past, you are creating your reality ahead of time." By understanding and consciously directing your frequency, you can align yourself with opportunities, relationships, and outcomes that resonate with your desires.

Your Frequency: The Energy You Emit

To understand the Law of Attraction, start by visualizing yourself as a magnet. What you draw into your life is a reflection of the energy you emit. When you dwell on joy, hope, and gratitude, you create a magnetic pull for experiences and relationships that mirror those emotions. Conversely, dwelling on fear, resentment, or doubt attracts obstacles and negativity.

Energy flows where attention goes. For example, if you continuously focus on debt, you emit a frequency of scarcity, unintentionally attracting more financial challenges. But if you shift your attention to abundance—the resources, opportunities, and blessings already in your life— your frequency changes, drawing more abundance into your experience. As Bob Doyle stated, "The Law of Attraction responds to your vibration, not your words."

The Science of Energy

Physics teaches us that energy is the building block of everything in the universe. From the smallest particle to the vastness of space, energy vibrates at different frequencies. Your thoughts and emotions, as extensions of this energy, also vibrate. This vibration interacts with the energetic field around you, shaping your reality.

Dr. Masaru Emoto's experiments with water crystals offer a fascinating glimpse into this phenomenon. Emoto exposed water to positive words like "love" and "gratitude," as well as negative ones like "hate." When frozen, the water exposed to positive words formed beautiful, intricate crystals, while the negatively charged water formed distorted patterns. This experiment demonstrates how vibrations—in the form of words and emotions—can impact physical matter.

On a neurological level, Dr. Joe Dispenza explains that your thoughts create measurable electromagnetic fields around your body. "Every thought you think sends a signal into the quantum field," he says. This signal, paired with the emotions you feel, acts as a blueprint for the reality you create.

Why Focus Matters

Your dominant thoughts act as a lens through which you perceive and interact with the world. For example:

- If you focus on the belief that "I'm not good enough," you'll unconsciously attract situations that reinforce this narrative.

- If you focus on gratitude and possibility, your brain's Reticular Activating System (RAS) will highlight opportunities aligned with those thoughts.

The RAS is a network of neurons in the brain that acts as a filter, helping you process information relevant to your focus. If you've ever bought a new car and suddenly noticed the same make and model everywhere, that's your RAS at work. Similarly, if you train your mind to focus on abundance, your RAS will attune itself to find opportunities that align with this belief.

The Role of Emotion in Shaping Frequency

Thoughts alone are not enough to activate the Law of Attraction. Emotion is the catalyst that amplifies your frequency. The universe doesn't respond to empty words; it responds to the feelings behind them. When you feel joy, gratitude, or excitement, you elevate your vibration, strengthening the signal you send out.

For instance, imagine visualizing a dream home. Simply thinking about it won't attract it into your life. But if you close your eyes and imagine yourself walking through the home, feeling the textures, hearing the sounds, and basking in the joy of ownership, you create a powerful emotional blueprint. This emotional charge is what draws the experience closer to you.

How to Consciously Direct Your Frequency

Harnessing the Law of Attraction requires intentional effort to align your thoughts, emotions, and actions. Here's how:

1. Cultivate Awareness

Pay attention to the thoughts and feelings that dominate your mind. Are they aligned with abundance, love, and possibility, or are they rooted in fear and doubt? Awareness is the first step toward change.

2. Reframe Limiting Beliefs

Replace disempowering beliefs with affirmations that reflect your desired reality. For example:

- Replace: "I'll never be successful."

- With: "Success flows to me effortlessly because I am aligned with my purpose."

3. Practice Gratitude

Gratitude is one of the most powerful tools for raising your vibration. By focusing on what you already have, you signal to the universe that you're ready to receive more.

Exercise: Each day, write down three things you're grateful for. Be specific. For instance, instead of writing, "I'm grateful for my health," try, "I'm grateful for the strength and energy I felt during my morning walk."

4. Visualize Your Goals

Spend 5–10 minutes daily visualizing your desires. Engage all your senses and imagine how achieving your goal will feel.

Example: If your goal is to start a business, imagine receiving your first positive review, hearing customers' gratitude, and feeling the pride of building something impactful.

5. Take Inspired Action

The Law of Attraction is not passive. Inspired action bridges the gap between intention and reality. Listen to your intuition and take steps that align with your goals.

Example: If you dream of becoming a writer, set aside time each day to work on your craft, submit your work to publishers, or join a writers' group.

The Power of Trusting the Process

Trust is a vital component of the Law of Attraction. Let go of attachment to specific outcomes and trust that the universe is working in your favor. This doesn't mean abandoning your goals; rather, it means releasing the anxiety and impatience that can lower your vibration.

Bob Doyle, another expert from *The Secret*, explains, "The Law of Attraction doesn't work on your timetable, but it works on the perfect timetable." Patience and trust create space for the universe to align circumstances in your favor.

Trusting the process involves surrendering control over how and when your desires will manifest. Instead of obsessing over results, focus on maintaining a high vibration and taking inspired action. This approach ensures that you remain open to opportunities and possibilities you might not have anticipated.

Mantra: "I trust that everything is unfolding perfectly, even if I can't see it right now." Repeat this mantra daily to reinforce your faith in the process.

Real-Life Transformation

Consider Mia, a single mother who dreamed of starting a wellness center but felt overwhelmed by her circumstances. She struggled with self-doubt, questioning whether she could balance her responsibilities and pursue her passion. Every evening, she would sit with her journal and write three things she was grateful for, even on her hardest days. Over time, this practice shifted her mindset from scarcity to possibility. She began to visualize her wellness center as a thriving, welcoming space filled with people benefiting from her services.

Mia's visualization practice became more detailed each day. She imagined the layout of her center, the vibrant energy of her clients, and the joy she felt helping others. This emotional connection to her dream elevated her vibrational frequency, creating a magnetic pull for opportunities.

One day, while sharing her vision with a friend, she was introduced to a mentor in the wellness industry. This mentor guided her through the process of crafting a business plan and encouraged her to apply for local small-business grants. Mia, once hesitant to ask for help, found herself receiving support from unexpected places. A community organization awarded her a grant, and her mentor helped her secure an affordable lease for her dream location.

Mia also began taking inspired action. She attended workshops on entrepreneurship, networked with professionals in her field, and started offering small wellness sessions in her local community. These steps not only built her confidence but also attracted more resources and connections. Within two years, her wellness center was thriving, a testament to the power of aligning thoughts, emotions, and actions.

Her story didn't end there. Mia continued to use the principles of the Law of Attraction to grow her business and maintain her high-frequency mindset. She expanded her offerings, introduced innovative wellness programs, and became a mentor to other aspiring entrepreneurs. Today, her center is not only a place of healing but also a beacon of inspiration for her community, demonstrating that even the most challenging circumstances can be transformed with focus, gratitude, and aligned action.

Mia's journey is just one example of how the Law of Attraction can create profound change. Another inspiring story is that of Jason, a freelance photographer who dreamed of turning his passion into a full-time career. For years, Jason felt stuck, believing he didn't have the connections or resources to succeed. After learning about the Law of Attraction, he began to shift his mindset.

Jason created a vision board filled with images of successful photo shoots, travel destinations, and inspiring quotes. Each day, he spent time visualizing himself capturing breathtaking moments, interacting with clients who valued his work, and receiving recognition for his talent. This daily practice not only elevated his mood but also gave him the clarity to pursue opportunities he had previously overlooked.

Within months, Jason began attracting clients who resonated with his vision. A chance meeting with a magazine editor led to his first major feature, and his portfolio quickly gained attention. By aligning his thoughts and actions, Jason turned his passion into a thriving career, proving that the Law of Attraction is a powerful tool for anyone willing to embrace it.

These stories show that transformation begins with a shift in perspective. Whether it's starting a business, pursuing a creative passion, or improving personal relationships, the Law of Attraction offers a framework for creating a life aligned with your deepest desires. By focusing on gratitude, visualizing success, and taking inspired action, you can overcome obstacles and achieve goals that once seemed out of reach.

Conclusion: A Life Transformed

The Law of Attraction is not just about achieving goals; it's about transforming how you perceive and interact with the world. By consciously directing your frequency, you become a magnet for the experiences and relationships that enrich your life. Remember, the universe responds to the energy you project, so choose thoughts and feelings that reflect the reality you wish to create.

In the next chapter, we'll explore how clarity and purpose amplify the power of the Law of Attraction, helping you define and manifest your most meaningful goals.

Part 2: Installing The Upgrade Code

Overview of Chapter 5: Clarity: Defining Your Definiteness of Purpose

Napoleon Hill identified *Definiteness of Purpose* as the starting point of all success. Without a clear, specific goal, your energy and efforts become scattered. Clarity brings focus, and focus brings results.

Why Clarity Matters

Imagine trying to hit a target you can't see. This is what happens when you pursue vague goals like "I want to be successful" or "I want to be happy." The subconscious mind thrives on specificity. The clearer your goal, the more effectively it works to achieve it.

How to Define Your Purpose

1. **Write It Down**: Put your goal into words. Be as specific as possible. Instead of "I want to lose weight," write, "I weigh 150 pounds by June 1."

2. **Visualize the Outcome**: Picture your goal as already achieved. What does it feel like? How does your life change?
3. **Align with Your Values**: Ensure your goal reflects your core values and passions. This alignment creates intrinsic motivation.

Clarity Exercise: The Life Map

- Divide a sheet of paper into sections: Health, Wealth, Relationships, Career, and Personal Growth.
- Write one clear, specific goal for each area.
- Review and refine these goals daily.

Chapter 5: Clarity: Defining Your Definiteness of Purpose

L ife's journey can be unpredictable and complex, filled with twists and turns that can leave even the most determined individuals feeling lost. Amid this uncertainty, clarity serves as a guiding compass, pointing you steadfastly toward the direction of your dreams. Without a clear sense of where you're going, it's easy to drift aimlessly, taking paths that lead to frustration, confusion, or stagnation. Goals without clarity become like ships without rudders, vulnerable to being tossed by the waves of life's challenges. Clarity, however, is more than a fleeting desire or vague ambition—it is the deliberate creation of a vivid, focused vision of your goals. It requires aligning your energy, thoughts, and actions to bring that vision into reality. With clarity, each decision and every action becomes a deliberate step closer to achieving your aspirations, creating momentum that propels you toward a life of purpose and fulfillment.

Napoleon Hill, in his timeless classic *Think and Grow Rich*, emphasized that Definiteness of Purpose is the cornerstone of all success. According to Hill, having a clear and unwavering goal serves as the foundation upon which achievement is built. He wrote, "There is one quality which one must possess to win, and that is definiteness of purpose, the knowledge of what one wants, and a burning desire to possess it." This burning desire is not a passive wish but a driving force that fuels persistence, determination, and creativity. It is the fire that propels individuals past challenges, distractions, and doubt. Hill further elaborates, "Success requires no apologies, and failure permits no alibis," underscoring the necessity of clarity in eliminating excuses and focusing solely on the pursuit of achievement.

Without clarity, even the most talented or resourceful individuals can find themselves spinning in circles, wasting energy on tasks that do not align with their true goals. Hill's insistence on a burning desire and definiteness of purpose challenges us to ask critical questions: *What do I truly want? Why does it matter to me? How will I achieve it?* When these questions are answered with clarity, they act as a beacon, illuminating the path to success even during the darkest moments.

Why Clarity is Essential for Success

Imagine embarking on a road trip to a destination you've never visited before. Without a map, GPS, or even a clear idea of where you're headed, the chances of arriving at your destination are slim. You might take wrong turns, waste valuable time, or end up in entirely the wrong place. Now imagine the same trip, but this time, you have a detailed itinerary, a clear map, and a working GPS. You know exactly where you're going, how long it will take, and what you'll experience along the way. The difference is night and day.

The same principle applies to life. Clarity acts as your personal roadmap, ensuring that your energy and efforts are channeled toward meaningful goals. Without it, you may find yourself working hard but achieving little, wondering why your dreams feel so far out of reach. When you have clarity, every step becomes purposeful, and every action aligns with your ultimate vision.

Hill's concept of Definiteness of Purpose highlights the transformative power of clarity. He observed that successful people not only know what they want but also create plans to achieve it, adjusting those plans as necessary without losing sight of their destination. Clarity helps you stay focused, motivated, and resilient in the face of obstacles. It eliminates distractions and prevents you from being pulled in too many directions at once, allowing you to concentrate your energy on what truly matters.

The Connection Between Clarity and the Subconscious Mind

Hill also recognized the profound role that the subconscious mind plays in turning clarity into reality. He explained that a clearly defined goal, repeated often enough, becomes deeply ingrained in the subconscious, where it works tirelessly to find solutions and opportunities. This process is akin to programming your mind with a success blueprint. Once the subconscious accepts the goal as an unwavering truth, it begins to align your thoughts, emotions, and actions with that vision, guiding you toward its fulfillment.

Consider the Reticular Activating System (RAS), a part of the brain that acts as a filter, highlighting information relevant to your focus. When you achieve clarity about your goals, your RAS helps you notice opportunities and resources that align with your vision, while filtering out distractions. For example, if your goal is to start a business, you may suddenly become more attuned to conversations, articles, and events related to entrepreneurship. This is not a coincidence; it's the power of clarity and focus at work.

The Role of Burning Desire

Hill's concept of a "burning desire" is inseparable from clarity. It's not enough to simply know what you want—you must feel an intense, almost obsessive passion for achieving it. This desire acts as fuel, sustaining you through setbacks, challenges, and delays. Without it, even the clearest goals can lose their luster over time, leaving you vulnerable to procrastination or discouragement.

A burning desire transforms ordinary goals into non-negotiable priorities. It compels you to take bold action, think creatively, and persist when others might give up. Hill wrote, "When a man really desires a thing so deeply that he is willing to stake his entire future on a single turn of the wheel in order to get it, he is sure to win." This level of commitment creates an unshakable belief in your ability to succeed, which is essential for attracting the resources and opportunities you need.

The Importance of Clarity

Clarity brings focus, and focus magnifies your ability to manifest your desires. When you're unclear about what you want, your energy is scattered, making it difficult for the universe to respond to your intentions. Think of it as placing an order at a restaurant. If you vaguely tell the waiter, "Bring me something to eat," you might end up with a dish you don't like. But when you clearly specify what you want, the likelihood of receiving exactly that increases exponentially.

The Benefits of Clarity

1. **Increased Motivation:** A clear goal ignites passion and drives you to take action. It becomes the "why" behind your efforts.

2. **Efficient Use of Energy:** When you know what you're aiming for, you can channel your time, energy, and resources more effectively.

3. **Reduced Stress:** Clarity eliminates confusion and indecision, creating a sense of purpose and direction.

4. **Faster Manifestation:** The universe responds to clear intentions. The more specific your vision, the easier it is to align your frequency with your goals.

Uncovering Your True Desires

Many people struggle with clarity because they're unsure of what they truly want. They may set goals based on societal expectations, family pressures, or fleeting desires rather than their authentic passions. To uncover your true desires, ask yourself:

- **What brings me joy?** Reflect on the activities, people, and experiences that make you feel alive and fulfilled.

- **What am I naturally drawn to?** Your interests and talents often hold clues to your purpose.

- **What legacy do I want to leave?** Consider how you want to impact the world and be remembered.

- **If I had no fear or limitations, what would I pursue?** Imagine a life where anything is possible and allow your heart to guide you.

Creating a Clear Vision

Once you've identified your true desires, the next step is to create a clear and detailed vision of your goal. This vision acts as a blueprint for your subconscious mind and the universe to follow. The more vivid and specific your vision, the stronger its magnetic pull.

How to Craft a Vision

1. **Be Specific:** Avoid vague statements like "I want to be successful." Instead, define what success looks like to you. For example, "I earn $10,000 per month doing work I love, helping people improve their health and well-being."

2. **Engage All Senses:** When visualizing your goal, include details that appeal to all your senses. What do you see, hear, smell, taste, and feel? The more vivid the imagery, the more real it becomes to your subconscious.

3. **Focus on the Emotion:** Emotion is the driving force behind manifestation. Imagine how achieving your goal will make you feel

—joyful, proud, grateful, or fulfilled. Let those emotions fuel your visualization.

4. **Write It Down:** Putting your vision into words solidifies it in your mind and makes it more tangible. Write a detailed description of your goal as if it has already happened.

Example of a Clear Vision

Imagine your goal is to start a successful online business. Your vision might look like this:

I wake up each morning excited to check my email, where I see messages from satisfied customers thanking me for the value I provide. My website, with its sleek design and user-friendly interface, attracts thousands of visitors each month. I earn $10,000 per month in passive income, allowing me to spend more time with my family and travel to beautiful destinations. I feel grateful, confident, and inspired to continue growing my business.

Aligning with Your Vision

Having a clear vision is the first step, but aligning your thoughts, emotions, and actions with that vision is equally important. Here's how:

1. Revisit Your Vision Daily

Spend a few minutes each morning and evening visualizing your goal as if it's already achieved. This keeps your vision at the forefront of your mind and reinforces your belief in its attainability.

2. Use Affirmations

Affirmations are positive statements that support your vision. For example, if your goal is to become financially independent, repeat affirmations like, "Money flows to me easily and abundantly" or "I am financially free and secure."

3. Take Inspired Action

Clarity helps you identify the steps needed to achieve your goal. Break your vision into smaller, actionable tasks and commit to taking consistent action. Listen to your intuition for guidance and remain open to opportunities that align with your purpose.

4. Surround Yourself with Support

Share your vision with supportive friends, family, or mentors who can encourage you and hold you accountable. Being part of a community that shares your values and goals amplifies your energy and motivation.

Common Obstacles to Clarity

Despite its importance, clarity can be surprisingly elusive. Many people struggle to define their goals with precision, often because they are influenced by fear, doubt, or external expectations. Here are some common obstacles to clarity and how to overcome them:

1. **Fear of Failure:** Fear can cloud your vision, making it difficult to set ambitious goals. To overcome this, remind yourself that failure is not the opposite of success—it's a stepping stone. Each setback provides valuable lessons that bring you closer to your goal.

2. **Overwhelm:** Big goals can feel daunting, leading to procrastination or paralysis. Break your vision into smaller, manageable steps and focus on one task at a time. Celebrate small wins to build momentum.

3. **External Influences:** Opinions from others can distract you from your true desires. Take time to reflect on what you truly want,

independent of societal or familial expectations.

4. **Lack of Belief:** Doubts about your abilities can prevent you from dreaming big. Use affirmations, visualization, and small successes to build confidence and reinforce your belief in your potential.

Practical Exercise: Defining Your Definiteness of Purpose

1. **Reflect:** Set aside 15 minutes in a quiet space. Write down your answers to the following questions:

   o   What do I truly want to achieve in the next 1, 5, or 10 years?

   o   Why is this goal important to me?

   o   How will achieving it make me feel?

2. **Create a Vision Statement:** Using your reflections, write a concise statement that summarizes your goal and the emotions it evokes. For example: *My purpose is to create a thriving wellness business that empowers others to live healthier lives while giving me the freedom and fulfillment I desire.*

3. **Visualize:** Close your eyes and imagine your goal as already achieved. Spend 5 minutes immersing yourself in the experience, engaging all your senses.

4. **Commit:** Write down three action steps you can take this week to move closer to your goal. Schedule them on your calendar and hold yourself accountable.

Real-Life Transformation Through Clarity

Clarity has the power to transform lives. Consider Sarah, a graphic designer who felt unfulfilled in her job but wasn't sure what she wanted to do next. After reading *Think and Grow Rich*, she decided to apply Hill's principles of Definiteness of Purpose. Through journaling and self-reflection, Sarah realized that her true passion was helping small businesses develop their brand identities.

With this newfound clarity, Sarah set a clear goal: to start her own branding agency within a year. She wrote a detailed vision statement describing her ideal clients, the services she would offer, and the joy she would feel running her own business. She revisited this vision daily, using visualization and affirmations to keep her focus sharp.

Despite challenges, Sarah's burning desire drove her to take bold steps. She attended networking events, built a portfolio, and secured her first few clients. Within a year, Sarah had successfully launched her agency, fulfilling a dream she once thought was impossible. Her story illustrates how clarity, combined with action and belief, can lead to extraordinary results.

The Power of Clarity

Clarity is the foundation of success and fulfillment. By defining your definiteness of purpose, you create a roadmap that guides your thoughts, emotions, and actions toward your goals. As you align with your vision and take inspired action, the universe responds, helping you manifest a life of purpose and abundance.

Clarity is not just a concept; it is a transformative force that can turn dreams into reality. By defining your goals with precision, cultivating a burning desire, and aligning your energy and actions, you create a powerful magnet for success. As Napoleon Hill so eloquently stated, "There are no limitations to the mind except those we acknowledge." With clarity as your compass, there are no limits to what you can achieve.

In the next chapter, we'll explore how to reprogram limiting beliefs and align your subconscious mind with your goals, ensuring lasting success and transformation.

Practical Exercise: Life Map

Step 1: Divide your life into categories: Health, Wealth, Relationships, Career, and Personal Growth.

Step 2: Write one clear, specific goal for each category.

Step 3: Rank your goals by priority. Which one will you focus on first?

Step 4: Create a timeline and action plan for your top goal.

Overcoming Common Challenges

- **Fear of Choosing the Wrong Goal**:
  Remember, clarity doesn't mean rigidity.
  You can adjust your path as you gain new
  insights.
- **Overwhelm**: Start small. Focus on one goal
  at a time to build momentum.

By defining your purpose, you take the first step
toward turning your dreams into reality.

Overview of Chapter 6: Reprogramming Beliefs

Your beliefs act as the operating system of your subconscious. They determine what you think is possible and shape the results you achieve. Many of these beliefs were formed in childhood and operate unconsciously, creating invisible barriers to success.

Identifying Limiting Beliefs

To reprogram your subconscious, you must first identify the beliefs holding you back. Common limiting beliefs include:

- "I'm not smart enough."
- "Money is hard to earn."
- "I don't deserve love."

Ask yourself:

- What do I believe about money, success, and relationships?
- Where did these beliefs come from?
- Are they serving me, or limiting me?

Rewriting Your Beliefs

1. **Challenge the Old Belief**: Question its validity. Is it true, or is it a story you've accepted as truth?
2. **Replace with a New Belief**: Create a new, empowering belief. For example, replace "Money is hard to earn" with "I attract money easily and effortlessly."
3. **Reinforce Through Repetition**: Use affirmations, visualization, and daily rituals to embed the new belief.

The Power of Emotional Rehearsal

Emotions act as the glue that binds beliefs to your subconscious. When rehearsing your new belief, feel the emotions associated with it—confidence, joy, gratitude. This accelerates the reprogramming process.

Chapter 6: Reprogramming Beliefs

Your beliefs shape your reality. They act as the lens through which you view the world and the blueprint your subconscious follows. Beliefs influence how you think, feel, and act, often operating beneath the surface of conscious awareness. If your beliefs are limiting, they act as barriers that hold you back from achieving your full potential. If they're empowering, they serve as a foundation that propels you forward. Reprogramming your beliefs is not just beneficial—it is essential for installing The Upgrade Code and transforming your life.

How Beliefs Are Formed

Beliefs don't appear out of nowhere. They are created through repetition, emotional experiences, and the influence of authority figures. Many of your core beliefs were established during childhood, when your mind was especially impressionable. At that age, your subconscious mind absorbed messages without critical analysis, creating foundational truths that continue to shape your thoughts and actions as an adult.

The Three Pathways to Belief Formation

1. **Repetition:** Messages repeated over time become internalized. For example, hearing phrases like "Money doesn't grow on trees" or "You're not good at math" can create limiting beliefs about wealth or intelligence.

2. **Emotional Experiences:** Events tied to strong emotions—such as failure, rejection, or success—leave a lasting impression on your subconscious.

3. **Authority Figures:** Parents, teachers, and other influential figures shape your belief system by modeling behaviors and communicating values.

Joseph Murphy, in *The Power of Your Subconscious Mind*, explains, "Your subconscious mind accepts what you feel as true. It does not argue with you." This highlights the importance of being mindful about the messages you internalize. What you speak to yourself, matters.

Identifying Limiting Beliefs

To reprogram your beliefs, you must first identify the ones that are holding you back. Limiting beliefs often hide in plain sight, disguised as self-doubt, procrastination, or fear. Here are three key strategies for uncovering them:

1. Examine Patterns

Look for recurring challenges in your life. Are there areas where you consistently feel stuck or frustrated? These patterns often point to underlying beliefs. For example, if you frequently struggle with relationships, you might hold a belief like, "I'm not worthy of love."

2. Pay Attention to Self-Talk

Your inner dialogue reveals a lot about your beliefs. Are your thoughts supportive or critical? Negative self-talk, such as "I'll never be successful," often stems from limiting beliefs.

3. Reflect on Your Past

Think about the messages you absorbed during childhood. Did your parents or caregivers reinforce ideas like, "You have to work hard to succeed," or "People like us don't get rich"? These early lessons may still be influencing your mindset today.

How to Reprogram Beliefs

Reprogramming your beliefs involves replacing limiting ones with empowering alternatives. This process requires awareness, intentionality, and repetition. Here's how to do it:

Step 1: Awareness

The first step is recognizing the limiting belief. Write it down and explore its origins. Ask yourself:

- Where did this belief come from?

- How has it impacted my life?

- Is it serving me or holding me back?

Step 2: Challenge the Belief

Question the validity of your belief. Limiting beliefs often crumble under scrutiny. Ask yourself:

- Is this belief absolutely true?

- What evidence contradicts it?

- How would my life change if I no longer held this belief?

Step 3: Replace the Belief

Create a new, empowering belief that aligns with your goals. For example:

- Replace: "I'm not good with money" with "I manage my finances with confidence and ease."

- Replace: "I'll never find love" with "I am deserving of a loving and fulfilling relationship."

Step 4: Reinforce Through Repetition

Use affirmations, visualization, and journaling to embed the new belief in your subconscious. Consistent repetition is key to rewiring your mind.

Step 5: Take Aligned Action

Act in ways that support your new belief. For instance, if your new belief is "I am a confident and capable leader," look for opportunities to take on leadership roles. Small wins reinforce the new mindset and build momentum.

Three Stories of Belief Transformation

Story 1: Overcoming Financial Limitation

Mark grew up in a household where money was always a source of stress. His parents often said, "We can't afford that," and "Rich people are greedy." As an adult, Mark struggled financially despite working hard. He realized he held a limiting belief: "I'll never be wealthy because money is bad."

Through self-reflection and journaling, Mark traced this belief back to his childhood. He began challenging it by asking, "Is money inherently bad?" and, "Can wealth be used for good?" He replaced his limiting belief with a new one: "Money is a tool that helps me create a positive impact."

To reinforce this belief, Mark started practicing gratitude for the money he already had and visualizing himself using wealth to support causes he cared about. He also took a financial literacy course to improve his money management skills. Over time, Mark's financial situation improved dramatically, and he developed a healthier relationship with money.

Story 2: Rebuilding Self-Worth

Jenna's self-esteem took a hit after a series of failed relationships. She internalized the belief, "I'm not worthy of love." This belief affected every area of her life, from her friendships to her career.

During a personal development workshop, Jenna confronted this limiting belief. She realized it was rooted in past experiences of rejection and criticism. She challenged the belief by asking, "What evidence proves I am unworthy?" and, "How can I show myself love and care?"

Jenna replaced her old belief with: "I am lovable and deserving of meaningful relationships." She reinforced this belief through daily affirmations and acts of self-care, such as journaling, meditating, and pursuing hobbies she enjoyed. Over time, Jenna's confidence grew, and she formed healthier, more fulfilling relationships.

Story 3: Transforming Fear into Confidence

Alex had always wanted to start his own business but was paralyzed by the belief, "I'm not good enough to succeed." This fear kept him stuck in a job he disliked, yearning for a change but too afraid to take action.

Through coaching, Alex identified the source of his belief: a critical teacher who had dismissed his ideas in school. He began challenging the belief by listing his accomplishments and skills, proving to himself that he was capable. He replaced the limiting belief with: "I have the skills and determination to build a successful business."

To reinforce this belief, Alex visualized himself running a thriving business and celebrated small wins, such as creating a business plan and securing his first client. Taking these steps helped Alex build confidence, and within a year, he left his job to pursue his entrepreneurial dreams.

The Power of Reprogramming Beliefs

Reprogramming your beliefs is like upgrading the software of your mind. It takes time, effort, and consistency, but the results are life-changing. As Joseph Murphy wrote, "Change your thoughts, and you change your destiny." By replacing limiting beliefs with empowering ones, you align your subconscious mind with your conscious goals, creating a powerful synergy that accelerates your growth and success.

In the next chapter, we'll explore how daily habits reinforce The Upgrade Code and help you create lasting transformation.

Practical Exercise: Belief Audit

1. **Choose an Area of Focus:** Identify one area of your life where you feel stuck, such as finances, relationships, or career.

2. **Identify the Limiting Belief:** Write down the belief that's holding you back. Be honest and specific.

3. **Create a New Belief:** Write a new, empowering belief that aligns with your goals.

4. **Reinforce the New Belief:** Practice affirmations, visualization, and journaling daily. Look for small actions you can take to support the new belief.

5. **Track Your Progress:** Monitor changes in your thoughts, feelings, and actions over time.

Overview of Chapter 7: Mastering Daily Habits

Habits are the building blocks of your life. They automate your actions, conserve energy, and shape your reality. Installing The Upgrade Code requires aligning your daily habits with your goals.

The Science of Habit Formation

Research shows it takes approximately 21–66 days to form a new habit. During this period, consistency is more important than intensity. Small, consistent actions create lasting change.

Creating High-Impact Habits

1. **Morning Rituals**: Start your day with practices that set a positive tone— meditation, affirmations, and goal review.
2. **Evening Reflection**: End your day with gratitude journaling and visualization.
3. **Anchor Habits**: Pair new habits with existing ones. For example, repeat affirmations while brushing your teeth.

The 1% Rule

Focus on improving by just 1% each day. Over time, these small improvements compound into remarkable results.

Chapter 7: Mastering Daily Habits

Habits are the building blocks of your life. They shape your daily actions, and your daily actions determine your long-term results. Whether they are supportive or destructive, habits hold incredible power over your personal transformation. As Joseph Murphy wrote in *The Power of Your Subconscious Mind*, "The subconscious mind is habit-bound. It follows the patterns you establish, good or bad." This chapter explores how to consciously craft and master habits that align with The Upgrade Code, creating a foundation for lasting success.

The Science of Habits

Habits form through a loop of cue, routine, and reward. A cue triggers the behavior, the routine is the behavior itself, and the reward reinforces it. This loop, once repeated often enough, becomes automatic and deeply ingrained in your subconscious mind. Understanding this process allows you to break negative habits and establish positive ones.

For example:

- **Cue:** You wake up in the morning.

- **Routine:** You reach for your phone and scroll through social media.

- **Reward:** You feel a temporary sense of distraction or connection.

By identifying and modifying each step in the habit loop, you can replace unhelpful routines with productive ones.

Why Habits Matter in Personal Transformation

Your habits are the silent architects of your life. They determine whether you consistently take action toward your goals or remain stuck in patterns that hold you back. As Murphy observed, "You are the sum total of your habits." To achieve meaningful change, you must align your habits with your vision and values.

Consider this analogy: If your goal is to climb a mountain, your habits are the steps that carry you upward. Small, consistent steps build momentum and make even the steepest climbs manageable.

Standard Operating Procedures for Creating Habits

Creating and maintaining positive habits requires intentionality and structure. Below is a step-by-step guide to building habits that last:

1. Identify Your Keystone Habits

Keystone habits are behaviors that have a ripple effect, positively influencing multiple areas of your life. Examples include:

- Morning routines that set the tone for the day.

- Daily exercise, which boosts energy and focus.

- Journaling, which fosters self-awareness and clarity.

Action Step: Reflect on your goals and identify one keystone habit that supports them. Start with this habit to maximize impact.

2. Start Small and Build Gradually

One of the most common mistakes when forming new habits is trying to change too much at once. Small, incremental changes are more sustainable and less overwhelming.

Example: If your goal is to meditate for 20 minutes daily, start with 2 minutes and gradually increase the duration over time.

Action Step: Break your desired habit into smaller steps and focus on consistency rather than perfection.

3. Anchor New Habits to Existing Routines

Pairing a new habit with an existing routine creates a natural cue for the behavior. This technique, known as habit stacking, makes it easier to integrate new habits into your daily life.

Example: After brushing your teeth, spend 5 minutes writing in your gratitude journal.

Action Step: Identify an existing routine you can use as a cue for your new habit.

4. Use Visualization and Affirmation

Visualization and affirmations help reprogram your subconscious mind to support your new habits. Imagine yourself performing the habit effortlessly and affirm your ability to maintain it.

Example: Visualize yourself waking up early, feeling energized, and completing your morning workout. Repeat affirmations like, "I am disciplined and consistent in my habits."

Action Step: Spend a few minutes each day visualizing your desired habit and reinforcing it with affirmations.

5. Create a Reward System

Rewards reinforce the habit loop by associating positive feelings with the behavior. These rewards can be intrinsic (a sense of accomplishment) or extrinsic (treating yourself to something enjoyable).

Example: After completing a week of consistent exercise, reward yourself with a relaxing massage or a favorite activity.

Action Step: Choose a meaningful reward that motivates you to stick with your habit.

6. Track Your Progress

Tracking your habits creates accountability and provides tangible evidence of your efforts. A habit tracker, journal, or app can help you monitor consistency.

Example: Use a calendar to mark off each day you complete your habit. Aim for streaks to build momentum.

Action Step: Choose a method to track your habits and review your progress regularly.

7. Plan for Obstacles

Anticipating challenges helps you stay committed when things don't go as planned. Identify potential obstacles and create strategies to overcome them.

Example: If you're traveling and can't visit the gym, plan to do a bodyweight workout in your hotel room instead.

Action Step: List potential obstacles to your habit and brainstorm solutions in advance.

8. Surround Yourself with Support

Your environment and social circle significantly influence your habits. Surround yourself with people who encourage your growth and create an environment that supports your goals.

Example: Join a group or community with similar goals, such as a running club or personal development forum.

Action Step: Identify one person or group who can support you in building your new habit.

The Role of Subconscious Reprogramming in Habits

Joseph Murphy emphasized the role of the subconscious mind in habit formation. He wrote, "As you sow in your subconscious mind, so shall you reap in your body and environment." By repeatedly planting positive suggestions and visualizing successful outcomes, you can reprogram your subconscious to support your desired habits.

For example, if you struggle with procrastination, you can affirm, "I take action promptly and consistently." Over time, these affirmations create new neural pathways that make prompt action your default behavior.

Real-Life Examples of Habit Transformation

1. The Morning Routine That Changed Everything

Emma, a busy professional, felt constantly overwhelmed and unproductive. She decided to create a morning routine to set a positive tone for her day. Starting small, Emma committed to waking up 15 minutes earlier to meditate and plan her priorities. As this habit became ingrained, she added journaling and light exercise to her routine. Within months, Emma noticed significant improvements in her focus, energy, and overall well-being. Her morning routine became the keystone habit that transformed her life.

2. Breaking the Cycle of Procrastination

David struggled with procrastination, often delaying important tasks until the last minute. After identifying his cue (feeling overwhelmed) and reward (temporary relief), he replaced his routine with a productive alternative. David began using the

Pomodoro Technique, working in focused 25-minute intervals followed by short breaks. He also visualized himself completing tasks efficiently and affirmed, "I tackle my work with focus and determination." This simple habit shift improved David's productivity and reduced his stress levels.

3. Building a Consistent Fitness Habit

Sophia had always wanted to exercise regularly but found it hard to stay consistent. She started by committing to 10 minutes of movement each day, such as walking or stretching. To reinforce the habit, Sophia stacked it with her existing evening routine, exercising right after dinner. She tracked her progress using a habit tracker and rewarded herself with a new workout outfit after completing 30 consecutive days. Over time, Sophia's 10-minute workouts grew into a daily hour-long fitness routine that became a natural part of her life.

Practical Exercise: Habit Blueprint

1. **Choose a Habit:** Identify one habit that aligns with your goals.

2. **Define the Habit Loop:** Write down the cue, routine, and reward for the habit.

3. **Create an Action Plan:** Use the Standard Operating Procedures outlined above to design your habit.

4. **Track Your Progress:** Use a habit tracker or journal to monitor consistency.

5. **Reflect and Adjust:** Review your progress regularly and make adjustments as needed.

The Compounding Power of Habits

Habits, like compound interest, grow in power over time. Small, consistent actions may seem insignificant at first, but they lead to exponential results. As Murphy observed, "Your subconscious mind works continuously while you are awake and while you sleep." By embedding positive habits into your subconscious, you create a system that works tirelessly to support your success.

Mastering daily habits is a cornerstone of The Upgrade Code. By following the strategies and principles in this chapter, you can build a life that reflects your highest potential, one habit at a time.

In the next chapter, we will explore the importance of community and connection in sustaining your growth and amplifying your results.

Practical Exercise: The 21-Day Habit Challenge

Step 1: Choose one habit that aligns with your goals.

Step 2: Identify a trigger and reward.

Step 3: Commit to practicing the habit daily for 21 days.

Step 4: Reflect on your progress and adjust as needed.

Overview of Chapter 8: The Mastermind

Napoleon Hill defined the Mastermind as a powerful alliance of individuals who come together to share ideas, provide mutual support, and accelerate each other's success. This timeless principle underscores the transformative power of collaboration in achieving meaningful goals.

The Power of Connection

A well-structured Mastermind network offers:

Accountability: Keeps you focused and dedicated to your goals through shared commitment.

Collective Wisdom: Provides diverse insights, innovative solutions, and fresh perspectives.

 Emotional Support: Fosters encouragement and resilience during challenges, creating a sense of shared purpose and community.

Chapter 8: The Mastermind

S uccess is rarely a solo journey. Throughout history, the greatest achievements have been the result of collaboration, guidance, and shared wisdom. As Napoleon Hill emphasized in *Think and Grow Rich*, "No two minds ever come together without thereby creating a third, invisible, intangible force, which may be likened to a third mind." This is the essence of a mastermind group— a powerful alliance of individuals united by a shared purpose, providing mutual support, accountability, and inspiration.

Mastermind groups, mentorships, and business networking circles serve as catalysts for personal and professional growth. Whether you're seeking advice, brainstorming solutions, or expanding your perspective, surrounding yourself with the right people can transform your trajectory. This chapter explores how to build and nurture a mastermind network tailored to your goals, harnessing the collective power of like-minded individuals to amplify your success.

The Concept of the Mastermind

Napoleon Hill described the mastermind as "the coordination of knowledge and effort, in a spirit of harmony, between two or more people, for the attainment of a definite purpose." The principle rests on the idea that collaboration generates synergy, producing results far greater than what any individual could achieve alone.

When you engage with a mastermind group, mentorship, or coaching circle, you gain access to:

- **Shared Knowledge:** Diverse perspectives and expertise enrich your understanding and problem-solving abilities.

- **Accountability:** Group members hold you to your commitments, ensuring steady progress.

- **Encouragement:** The collective energy of the group inspires you to persevere through challenges.

- **Opportunities:** Networking opens doors to partnerships, resources, and collaborations.

The Power of Surrounding Yourself with the Right People

Hill observed that your "mental environment" directly influences your success. He wrote, "You are the average of the five people you spend the most time with." This highlights the importance of curating your circle carefully. Positive, growth-oriented individuals uplift and motivate you, while negative or complacent influences can hinder your progress.

To create a supportive environment, consider:

- **Mentorship:** Seek guidance from someone more experienced who can share their wisdom and help you navigate challenges.

- **Coaching:** Engage with a professional coach who provides personalized strategies and accountability.

- **Business Networking:** Join industry groups, roundtables, or professional associations to connect with peers and experts.

- **Support Groups:** Surround yourself with people who understand your struggles and can provide encouragement and solidarity.

Building Your Mastermind Network

Creating a mastermind network requires intentionality. Follow these steps to form a group that aligns with your goals:

1. Define Your Purpose

Start by clarifying the purpose of your mastermind group. What do you hope to achieve? Whether it's advancing your career, launching a business, or improving a specific skill, a clear objective ensures alignment among members.

Example: If you're an entrepreneur, your group's purpose might be to share strategies for scaling businesses, navigating market trends, or managing teams effectively.

2. Choose the Right Members

Select individuals who share your values and commitment to growth. Diversity in skills and experiences enriches the group, but mutual respect and a collaborative mindset are essential.

Qualities to Look For:

- Expertise or knowledge relevant to the group's goals.

- A willingness to give as much as they receive.

- Positive energy and a growth-oriented mindset.

Action Step: Identify 3-5 people whose strengths complement yours and invite them to join.

3. Establish Ground Rules

Clear guidelines create structure and ensure the group operates smoothly. Discuss:

- Meeting frequency (e.g., weekly, biweekly, or monthly).

- Meeting format (e.g., in-person, virtual, or hybrid).

- Confidentiality agreements to foster trust.

Example: Each meeting could include updates from members, a focused discussion on a specific challenge, and brainstorming sessions for solutions.

4. Foster a Collaborative Environment

Encourage open communication, active listening, and constructive feedback. Each member should feel valued and heard.

Tips for Collaboration:

- Rotate leadership roles or meeting facilitators.

- Use structured agendas to maximize productivity.

- Celebrate milestones and achievements to maintain motivation.

Leveraging Mentorship and Coaching

Mentorship and coaching are invaluable components of a successful mastermind network. They provide tailored guidance and insights based on firsthand experience.

The Role of a Mentor

A mentor is someone who has walked the path you aspire to follow. They offer:

- **Wisdom:** Sharing lessons learned from their own successes and failures.

- **Perspective:** Providing an objective view of your challenges and opportunities.

- **Support:** Encouraging you to pursue your goals with confidence.

How to Find a Mentor:

- Join professional associations or attend industry events.

- Reach out to respected individuals in your field.

- Offer value in return, such as assistance on projects or sharing your own expertise.

The Value of Coaching

A coach helps you unlock your potential by focusing on your strengths, identifying blind spots, and creating actionable plans. Unlike mentors, who share their experience, coaches guide you to find your own solutions.

Benefits of Coaching:

- Clarity on your goals and priorities.

- Strategies for overcoming obstacles and building momentum.

- Accountability to keep you on track.

Action Step: Research certified coaches in your field or explore coaching programs that align with your needs.

Real-Life Examples of Mastermind Success

1. The Entrepreneur's Roundtable

Rachel, a small business owner, joined a local entrepreneur's roundtable to expand her network and gain insights. The group met biweekly to discuss marketing strategies, financial management, and industry trends. Through these meetings, Rachel gained valuable advice on scaling her operations and connected with a fellow member who became her business partner. Within a year, her revenue doubled, and her confidence as a leader grew.

2. The Support Group That Fostered Resilience

After facing a major career setback, James felt isolated and discouraged. A friend invited him to a support group for professionals navigating transitions. The group provided a safe space to share experiences and brainstorm solutions. Through the group's encouragement, James rebuilt his confidence, refined his skills, and secured a new role that aligned with his passions.

3. The Creative Mastermind

Sofia, a freelance graphic designer, struggled with creative blocks and inconsistent income. She formed a mastermind group with other creatives, including writers, photographers, and marketers. The group met monthly to share ideas, critique each other's work, and collaborate on projects. Over time, Sofia's creativity flourished, and her network of collaborators helped her attract high-profile clients.

Practical Exercise: Build Your Mastermind Network

1. **Identify Your Goal:** What do you hope to achieve through your mastermind group or mentorship? Write down a clear objective.

2. **List Potential Members:** Identify 3-5 people who could contribute to and benefit from the group.

3. **Initiate Contact:** Reach out to these individuals with a clear invitation, explaining the group's purpose and benefits.

4. **Set the First Meeting:** Schedule an initial session to establish goals, ground rules, and a meeting schedule.

5. **Evaluate and Adjust:** After a few sessions, gather feedback to improve the group's structure and effectiveness.

The Compounding Effect of Connection

The power of a mastermind network lies in its ability to amplify your efforts and accelerate your progress. As Hill wrote, "Power is organized knowledge expressed through intelligent effort." By surrounding yourself with a supportive, growth-oriented community, you tap into collective wisdom and create a powerful feedback loop of inspiration and accountability.

Investing in relationships with mentors, coaches, and peers not only enhances your personal and professional growth but also enriches your life with connection and collaboration. The people you surround yourself with become your greatest allies on the path to success.

In the next chapter, we will explore how to overcome resistance and doubt, equipping you with the tools to navigate challenges and stay aligned with your goals.

Part 3: Living the Upgrade Code

Overview of Chapter 9: Overcoming Resistance and Doubt

No matter how well you prepare, resistance and doubt will inevitably arise. These challenges are not signs of failure but opportunities to strengthen your commitment to transformation. As Napoleon Hill said, "Strength and growth come only through continuous effort and struggle."

Understanding Resistance

Resistance often stems from fear—fear of failure, fear of success, or fear of change. Your subconscious, programmed to maintain the status quo, may resist new beliefs and habits because it perceives them as threats.

Identifying Doubt

Doubt manifests as inner criticism, second-guessing, or hesitation. Left unchecked, it can derail your progress. To overcome doubt, it's crucial to distinguish between legitimate concerns and self-imposed limitations.

Tools to Overcome Resistance and Doubt

1. **Awareness**: Notice when resistance arises. Label it as a natural part of growth rather than a barrier.
2. **Reframe Negative Thoughts**: Turn "I can't do this" into "I'm learning how to do this."
3. **Take Small Steps**: Action dissolves fear. Even the smallest step forward builds confidence.
4. **Trust the Process**: Remember that growth is nonlinear. Trust that the principles of The Upgrade Code are working, even if progress seems slow.

Chapter 9: Overcoming Resistance and Doubt

Resistance and doubt are inevitable companions on the journey to personal growth and success. While external obstacles can often be identified and addressed, internal resistance—manifesting as self-doubt, fear, or limiting beliefs—requires a deeper level of self-awareness and effort to overcome. As Joseph Murphy explains in *The Power of Your Subconscious Mind*, "Your subconscious mind does not argue with you. It accepts what your conscious mind decrees. If you say, 'I can't do it,' your subconscious works to make it true." Overcoming self-doubt is a critical step in reprogramming your mind for success.

Bob Proctor, a key figure in the field of personal development, echoes this sentiment, emphasizing that self-doubt is not an inherent trait but a learned behavior rooted in childhood experiences. "Doubt and fear are mental diseases that disintegrate courage and self-reliance," Proctor explains. By addressing self-doubt at its core, you can unlock a mindset that empowers you to move beyond resistance and embrace your full potential.

Self-Doubt: A Version of Fear

At its core, self-doubt is a form of fear—a fear of failure, rejection, or inadequacy. It often stems from foundational beliefs established in childhood. For example, a child who is frequently criticized may internalize the belief that they are not good enough. These early messages are absorbed by the subconscious mind and replayed throughout life, creating a persistent undercurrent of doubt.

How Childhood Beliefs Shape Self-Doubt

- **Parental Criticism:** Repeated criticism from parents or authority figures can instill a belief that perfection is required to be accepted or loved.

- **Comparisons:** Being compared unfavorably to siblings or peers may lead to feelings of inadequacy.

- **Early Failures:** Negative experiences, such as struggling in school or sports, can form the belief that success is unattainable.

Joseph Murphy explains that these early influences become entrenched in the subconscious mind, acting as barriers to success. "The only thing that can hold you back is the fear of failure," he writes. Recognizing that self-doubt is learned, not innate, is the first step toward overcoming it.

Breaking Free from Self-Doubt

Overcoming self-doubt requires challenging its validity and replacing it with empowering beliefs. Both Joseph Murphy and Bob Proctor provide actionable strategies to help you dismantle self-doubt and rebuild confidence.

1. Recognize Self-Doubt as a Learned Pattern

Understanding that self-doubt is not an inherent part of who you are but a learned response allows you to separate yourself from it. Murphy advises, "Never finish a negative statement. Reverse it immediately and wonders will happen in your life." For example, if you find yourself thinking, "I'm not good enough," immediately counter it with, "I am capable and deserving of success."

Example: Sarah grew up in a family where academic success was highly valued. Despite her achievements, she felt inadequate because she believed she could never meet her parents' high expectations. By acknowledging this pattern and affirming, "I define my worth by my own standards, not others' expectations," Sarah began to free herself from self-doubt.

2. Use Visualization to Reprogram Beliefs

Visualization is a powerful tool for overcoming self-doubt. By vividly imagining yourself succeeding, you create a mental blueprint that your subconscious mind works to actualize. Bob Proctor emphasizes the importance of creating a clear and detailed mental image of your desired outcome. "See yourself already in possession of the goal. Hold that image firmly and consistently," Proctor advises.

Exercise: Close your eyes and visualize a situation where you previously felt doubt. Imagine yourself confidently succeeding in that scenario. Engage all your senses to make the visualization as vivid as possible. Repeat this exercise daily to reprogram your subconscious mind.

3. Reframe Failure as Growth

Self-doubt often arises from a fear of failure. Shifting your perspective on failure can help you overcome this fear. Murphy suggests viewing failure as feedback, a necessary step on the path to success. Similarly, Proctor encourages individuals to see failure as an opportunity to learn and grow.

Example: Mark, an aspiring entrepreneur, hesitated to launch his business because he feared it might fail. By reframing failure as a learning experience, he reminded himself that each setback was an opportunity to improve. This mindset shift allowed him to take action, refine his strategies, and eventually build a thriving business.

4. Develop a Habit of Affirmation

Affirmations are a cornerstone of both Murphy's and Proctor's teachings. They help you replace negative self-talk with positive, empowering statements. Affirmations should be specific, present-tense, and emotionally charged.

Examples of Affirmations:

- "I am worthy of success and abundance."

- "I trust my abilities to navigate challenges."

- "I am confident and capable in all that I do."

Exercise: Write down three affirmations that counter your most persistent doubts. Repeat them aloud every morning and night for 21 days to create lasting change.

5. Surround Yourself with Supportive Influences

Your environment plays a significant role in shaping your beliefs. Surrounding yourself with supportive, growth-oriented individuals can help you overcome self-doubt. Proctor emphasizes the importance of being part of a mastermind group or seeking mentorship to build confidence.

Example: Jenna joined a professional networking group to connect with like-minded peers. The encouragement and advice she received from the group boosted her confidence and helped her overcome doubts about her capabilities.

Real-Life Stories of Overcoming Self-Doubt

1. Breaking Free from "I'm Not Smart Enough"

Alex struggled with the belief that he wasn't smart enough to succeed in his chosen field. This doubt stemmed from a childhood teacher who had labeled him as "average." Through visualization and affirmations, Alex began to see himself as capable and intelligent. He consistently affirmed, "I am capable of mastering anything I set my mind to." Over time, Alex's confidence grew, and he earned a promotion that recognized his expertise and dedication.

2. Overcoming Impostor Syndrome

Maya, a recent graduate, landed her dream job but felt like an impostor among her more experienced colleagues. She constantly doubted her abilities, fearing she would be "found out." By working with a mentor and practicing affirmations like, "I belong here and contribute value," Maya gradually overcame her impostor syndrome. Her newfound confidence allowed her to excel and earn the respect of her peers.

3. Transforming "I Can't Handle Pressure"

David's belief that he couldn't handle pressure kept him from pursuing leadership roles. With the help of a coach, David identified this belief as a product of early experiences where he had been criticized for mistakes. By visualizing himself remaining calm and composed under pressure and affirming, "I thrive in challenging situations," David reprogrammed his subconscious. He soon took on a managerial position and excelled under the demands of leadership.

Practical Exercise: Rewriting Self-Doubt

1. **Identify a Doubt:** Write down one self-doubt that has been holding you back.

2. **Trace Its Origin:** Reflect on where this belief came from. Was it influenced by a specific event or person?

3. **Challenge Its Validity:** Ask yourself, "Is this belief absolutely true?" Look for evidence that contradicts it.

4. **Create an Affirmation:** Replace the limiting belief with a positive statement that reflects your true potential.

5. **Visualize Success:** Spend 5 minutes daily visualizing yourself overcoming the doubt and achieving your goal.

6. **Take Aligned Action:** Choose one small step that demonstrates your new belief in action. Repeat this process to build confidence over time.

Turning Doubt into Determination

Self-doubt may stem from childhood conditioning or past experiences, but it does not have to define your future. By recognizing self-doubt as a learned behavior, challenging its validity, and replacing it with empowering beliefs, you can transform resistance into resilience. As Joseph Murphy writes, "You can build radiant health, success, and happiness by the thoughts you think in the hidden studio of your mind." Through visualization, affirmations, and action, you reprogram your subconscious to support your highest potential. With persistence and trust in the process, doubt can become a stepping stone to greatness.

Chapter 10: The Master Code: Mindset Transformation, Gratitude, and Living Fully in the Present

The journey toward personal and professional fulfillment culminates in one profound realization: transformation happens in the present moment. This moment. The upgrade code is the *Master Code.* The ultimate blueprint for aligning your mindset, harnessing gratitude, and embracing the power of now. This final code programs a cohesive framework for unlocking your best life.

The Mindset Shift: From Limitation to Transformation

Your mindset determines the trajectory of your life. As Bob Proctor famously stated, "Your paradigm— your mental programming—dictates your results." Shifting from a mindset of limitation to one of growth and transformation begins with recognizing the power of your thoughts.

Napoleon Hill wrote, "Whatever the mind can conceive and believe, it can achieve." This truth underscores the importance of mastering your inner dialogue. Negative thoughts and doubts often stem from deeply ingrained beliefs, but they can be reprogrammed to align with your goals. Joseph Murphy emphasized this in *The Power of Your Subconscious Mind*: "Your subconscious mind takes the orders you give it based on your habitual thinking. If you choose positivity, you will draw positivity into your life."

Transformational Practices for Shifting Your Mindset

1. **Daily Affirmations:** Begin each day by affirming your goals and capabilities. Statements like "I am worthy of abundance" or "I am confident and capable" help rewire your subconscious mind.

2. **Visualization:** Close your eyes and vividly imagine yourself living your ideal life. Engage all your senses to make the experience feel real.

3. **Reframe Challenges:** Shift your perspective on obstacles, seeing them as opportunities for growth rather than setbacks.

Example: Sarah, a professional stuck in a repetitive job, reframed her dissatisfaction as a sign she was ready for a change. Through affirmations and visualization, she envisioned herself excelling in a more fulfilling career. This shift in mindset gave her the confidence to seek new opportunities, leading to a promotion and greater job satisfaction.

The Power of Gratitude

Gratitude is a force that transforms ordinary moments into extraordinary opportunities. Rhonda Byrne, in *The Secret*, explains, "Gratitude will shift you to a higher frequency, and you will attract much better things." By focusing on what you already have, you create an energetic alignment that attracts more of what you desire.

Why Gratitude Works

Gratitude rewires the brain to focus on abundance. It activates the reward centers of the brain, releasing dopamine and serotonin—the chemicals associated with happiness. Joseph Murphy noted, "The grateful heart draws great things to itself. Gratitude is a magnet for miracles."

Gratitude in Action

1. **Gratitude Journaling:** Write down three things you are grateful for every morning. Be specific and reflective.

2. **Gratitude Visualization:** Close your eyes and imagine your life as it is now. Feel deep appreciation for everything you've achieved, no matter how small.

3. **Express Gratitude:** Verbally thank the people, opportunities, and even challenges that contribute to your growth.

Example: John, who struggled with financial insecurity, began practicing gratitude daily. By appreciating his current resources and opportunities, he shifted his focus from scarcity to abundance. This shift opened his mind to possibilities he hadn't noticed before, eventually leading to a lucrative business venture.

Living Fully in the Present: The Power of Now

Eckhart Tolle's teachings in *The Power of Now* highlight the profound impact of living in the present moment. "Realize deeply that the present moment is all you ever have. Make the Now the primary focus of your life," Tolle advises. Living fully in the present frees you from the regrets of the past and the anxieties of the future, allowing you to take inspired action and experience true peace.

Why the Present Moment is Key

The present is the only time where creation and transformation occur. When you live fully in the Now, you:

- Release resistance to life as it unfolds.

- Align your energy with your goals.

- Access clarity and intuition, which guide your decisions.

Strategies for Embracing the Now

1. **Mindfulness Practices:** Engage fully in your current activity, whether it's working, eating, or spending time with loved ones.

2. **Breath Awareness:** Use your breath as an anchor to the present. Each inhale and exhale reconnects you with the moment.

3. **Acceptance:** Let go of the need to control every outcome. Trust that life unfolds as it should.

Example: Maria, a writer plagued by perfectionism, found peace by practicing mindfulness. Instead of worrying about the end product, she focused on the joy of writing in the present. Her work improved, and she experienced newfound creativity.

The Synergy of the Master Code

The Master Code is the harmonious integration of mindset, gratitude, and presence. Together, these principles create a life of abundance, purpose, and fulfillment. Napoleon Hill wrote, "You have absolute control over just one thing, your thoughts. This divine prerogative is the sole means by which you may control your destiny." By mastering your thoughts, embracing gratitude, and living fully in the present, you unlock the infinite potential within you.

Real-Life Stories of Transformation

1. The Executive Who Rediscovered Balance

Tom, a high-level executive, felt burned out and disconnected from his goals. Through mentorship and gratitude practice, he began focusing on the present and appreciating his achievements. This shift reignited his passion for work, improved his relationships, and brought newfound joy to his life.

2. The Single Mother Who Created Abundance

Maya, a single mother, used gratitude and visualization to transform her mindset. By joining a supportive mastermind group and taking inspired action, she built a thriving business that provided stability and freedom for her family.

3. The Artist Who Found Creative Flow

Sofia, an artist, often doubted her talent. By practicing mindfulness and affirming her creative abilities, she rediscovered the joy of creating. Her work flourished, and she gained recognition for her unique vision.

Practical Exercise: Activating the Master Code

1. **Mindset Reprogramming:** Identify a limiting belief and replace it with an empowering affirmation.

2. **Gratitude Ritual:** Write three things you're grateful for each day and reflect on their significance.

3. **Present Awareness:** Set aside 10 minutes daily to practice mindfulness or breath awareness.

4. **Visualize Your Dream Life:** Spend 5 minutes imagining your ideal future while feeling gratitude for the present.

Your Freedom - The Life of Your Dreams

The Master Code is your key to living a life of purpose, abundance, and joy. By mastering your mindset, cultivating gratitude, and living fully in the Now, you align yourself with the infinite possibilities of the universe. As Joseph Murphy reminds us, "Change your thoughts, and you change your destiny." With these tools, you hold the power to design a life that reflects your highest aspirations. The journey begins now, in this moment. Your extraordinary future awaits.

Go Master Your Life

The Upgrade Code is more than a system—it's a way of life. By mastering your subconscious mind, aligning your energy, and taking inspired action, you can create a reality that reflects your highest potential.

Transformation is a journey, not a destination. There will be setbacks, doubts, and challenges along the way, but each one is an opportunity to grow stronger, wiser, and more aligned. Trust the process, stay committed, and remember: you already have everything you need to succeed within you.

You are the programmer of your mind, the architect of your destiny, and the master of your life. It's time to install The Upgrade Code, rewrite your story, and live the extraordinary life you deserve.

The Significance of the 21-Day Challenge in The Upgrade Code Process

Throughout *The Upgrade Code*, the concept of a 21-day challenge is woven into various practices, offering a clear, actionable framework for reprogramming beliefs, building habits, and fostering transformation. The number 21 holds significance because in this authors opinion from research, it represents the approximate time it takes for the brain to begin forming new neural pathways and embedding a behavior or belief into the subconscious mind. As Joseph Murphy explained, "Repetition of the same thought or physical action develops a habit in the mind, which then becomes an automatic response." This period of repetition and consistency is vital to effectively installing The Upgrade Code. The 21-day challenge is a cornerstone of The Upgrade Code because it encapsulates the process of conscious repetition, focus, and transformation. By committing to this simple yet powerful framework, you take the first critical steps toward rewiring your subconscious mind and aligning your habits with your dreams. As Joseph Murphy said, "Constant repetition carries conviction. Repeat it regularly, and your subconscious mind will believe it." Through consistent practice over 21 days, you unlock the keys to lasting change, living fully in the present, and creating the life you desire.

Why 21 Days?

The idea that 21 days can create lasting change originates from studies in psychology and neuroscience, which show that habit formation and belief reprogramming require consistent repetition to establish new neural connections. When you engage in a behavior or thought process repeatedly over 21 days, your brain starts to rewire itself, reinforcing the behavior as a default pattern. This aligns with the teachings in *Think and Grow Rich*, where Napoleon Hill emphasized, "Persistence is the sustained effort necessary to induce faith." Consistency over three weeks builds the persistence needed to shift deeply rooted beliefs and habits.

The 21-Day Challenge Across the Book

1. **Reprogramming Beliefs (Chapter 6):** In this chapter, the 21-day framework is introduced as a method to overwrite limiting beliefs. By repeating affirmations like, "I am capable of achieving my dreams," paired with visualization, you actively train your subconscious to accept new truths. Bob Proctor's assertion that "repetition reprograms the subconscious" underscores the importance of daily practice during this critical period.

2. **Mastering Daily Habits (Chapter 7):** Creating lasting habits involves leveraging the 21-day challenge as a way to focus on one habit at a time, ensuring it becomes second nature. As discussed, starting small and maintaining consistency ensures that by the end of the three weeks, the habit is embedded deeply into your routine.

3. **Gratitude Practice (Master Code):** The 21-day challenge also serves as a gateway to cultivating gratitude. Writing down three things you're grateful for each day during this period helps shift your focus from lack to abundance, transforming your mindset and vibration in alignment with The Law of Attraction.

4. **Mindset Transformation (Chapters 1-3):** The book frequently emphasizes the role of visualization and affirmations. Practicing these techniques over a 21-day span helps you establish a clear mental image of your goals, enabling your subconscious to work in harmony with your conscious intentions.

Why 21 Days is Essential to The Upgrade Code Process

The Upgrade Code isn't about making surface-level adjustments; it's about creating lasting transformation. The 21-day challenge offers:

- **Structure:** It provides a tangible timeline to focus your efforts, ensuring you remain consistent.

- **Momentum:** Completing the challenge builds confidence and motivates you to continue.

- **Neurological Integration:** Repeated actions during this time period help form new neural pathways, making your desired beliefs and behaviors automatic.

How to Embark on Your Own 21-Day Challenge

1. **Set a Clear Intention:** Choose one specific belief or habit to focus on during the challenge.

2. **Commit to Daily Practice:** Whether it's affirmations, visualization, journaling, or gratitude, dedicate at least 5-10 minutes daily.

3. **Track Your Progress:** Use a journal or calendar to mark each day you complete the challenge, reinforcing your commitment.

4. **Celebrate Small Wins:** Acknowledge your effort and progress along the way, building confidence and motivation.

Core Concepts and Thought Leaders

The book draws on a variety of influential authors, thinkers, and concepts that have shaped its foundational ideas:

Joseph Murphy

The Power of Your Subconscious Mind
Central to understanding the subconscious as the operating system of the mind, Murphy's work emphasizes mental reprogramming through belief and positive thinking.

Napoleon Hill

Think and Grow Rich
Key contributor to the book's focus on Definiteness of Purpose, faith, and visualization for achieving success.

Wallace Wattles

The Science of Getting Rich
Introduced the systematic use of focused thought
and gratitude as mechanisms for manifesting
abundance.

Émile Coué

Autosuggestion Pioneer
Best known for popularizing the affirmation: *"Every
day, in every way, I am getting better and better."*
His work influenced the book's methods for
reprogramming limiting beliefs.

Rhonda Byrne

The Secret
Byrne's work on the Law of Attraction underpins
the book's discussions of energy alignment,
vibrational frequencies, and intentional
manifestation.

Eckhart Tolle

The Power of Now
Tolle's teachings on mindfulness, presence, and overcoming ego-driven thinking provide a foundation for emotional alignment and the importance of living in the present moment.

Dr. Joe Dispenza

Breaking the Habit of Being Yourself
Explains the neuroscience of thought patterns and their role in creating new realities. His work supports the book's focus on neuroplasticity and visualization.

Dr. Masaru Emoto

The Hidden Messages in Water
Demonstrated the impact of emotions and intention on physical matter, symbolizing the power of vibrational energy.

Philosophical and Historical Influences

The book incorporates wisdom from ancient and philosophical traditions:

The Upanishads

Emphasizes the creative power of thought and the unity between the mind and the universe.

The Emerald Tablet

A Hermetic text that explores the principles of mental and energetic alignment in shaping reality.

Psychological Frameworks and Techniques

The book adapts established psychological principles and practical tools:

Reticular Activating System (RAS)

A neuroscience concept that explains how focus and clarity influence perception and behavior.

Visualization and Emotional Amplification

Techniques widely used in sports psychology and personal development to strengthen neural pathways and build belief systems.

Neuroplasticity

The brain's ability to rewire itself through repeated thought patterns and emotional experiences, central to the book's reprogramming methods.

Terminology Reference Guide

This section provides definitions and explanations of key terminology used in *The Upgrade Code: Hack Your Software and Master Your Life* by Joshua J. Bowen. The guide ensures clarity and helps readers better understand the concepts discussed throughout the book.

1. Subconscious Mind

The part of the mind operating below conscious awareness. It stores beliefs, emotions, habits, and memories, and influences behaviors and decisions without deliberate thought. The subconscious acts as the "operating system" of your mind, as described in the book.

2. Autosuggestion

The process of reprogramming the subconscious mind by repeatedly feeding it positive, present-tense affirmations. Pioneered by Émile Coué, autosuggestion is a key tool for replacing limiting beliefs with empowering ones.

3. Visualization

A mental practice of creating detailed and emotionally vivid images of desired outcomes. By imagining success in specific scenarios, visualization helps reprogram the subconscious and aligns actions with goals.

4. Neuroplasticity

The brain's ability to reorganize and form new neural connections in response to repeated thoughts, behaviors, or experiences. This concept supports the idea that beliefs and habits can be changed through intentional mental reprogramming.

5. Reticular Activating System (RAS)

A network of neurons in the brain that filters information and highlights what is most relevant to your focus or goals. The RAS is influenced by your subconscious beliefs and plays a role in noticing opportunities aligned with your intentions.

6. Law of Attraction

A principle stating that thoughts and emotions emit energetic vibrations that attract corresponding experiences. It emphasizes the importance of maintaining a positive mindset and aligning energy with desired outcomes.

7. Limiting Beliefs

Deep-seated, often unconscious beliefs that constrain your potential or block progress. Examples include "I'm not good enough" or "Success is for others, not me." The book outlines methods to identify and replace these beliefs.

8. Vibrational Frequency

The energetic state created by your thoughts, emotions, and intentions. High-frequency vibrations, such as joy and gratitude, attract positive outcomes, while low-frequency vibrations, like fear and resentment, can hinder progress.

9. Emotional Amplification

The process of intensifying affirmations, visualizations, or beliefs by pairing them with strong, positive emotions. This helps embed desired outcomes into the subconscious more effectively.

10. Definiteness of Purpose

A concept introduced by Napoleon Hill, referring to having a clear and specific goal or vision. It is described in the book as the cornerstone of success, providing focus and direction for your efforts.

11. Burning Desire

A deep and passionate longing to achieve a goal or outcome. As emphasized in the book, a burning desire fuels persistence and action, even in the face of challenges.

12. Conscious Mind

The part of the mind responsible for logical thinking, planning, and decision-making. It inputs commands to the subconscious mind, acting as the "keyboard and mouse" of your mental computer.

13. Faith

A state of unwavering belief in your ability to succeed or in the realization of a goal. The book highlights faith as a mental and emotional foundation for overcoming doubts and obstacles.

14. Gratitude Practice

A daily habit of acknowledging and appreciating the positive aspects of life. Gratitude raises your vibrational frequency and aligns your energy with abundance and success.

15. Mental Reprogramming

The intentional process of replacing old, limiting mental patterns with new, empowering beliefs and behaviors. Techniques like autosuggestion, visualization, and journaling are used to facilitate reprogramming.

16. Inspired Action

Steps taken in alignment with your goals that feel purposeful and intuitive. Inspired action bridges the gap between intention and manifestation, combining effort with trust in the process.

17. Energy Alignment

The practice of aligning thoughts, emotions, and actions with your desired outcomes. When your energy aligns with your goals, you attract circumstances and opportunities that support them.

18. Scarcity Mindset

A belief system that focuses on lack and limitations, such as "There's never enough money." The book emphasizes shifting to an abundance mindset for personal transformation.

19. Emotional Anchoring

Attaching positive emotions, such as joy or gratitude, to new beliefs or visualizations to make them more impactful and memorable.

20. Practical Exercises

Step-by-step activities provided throughout the book to help readers implement concepts like visualization, autosuggestion, and goal setting. Examples include creating a vision board or writing affirmations.

Supplementary Materials

Worksheets and Guides available at www.TheUpgradeCode.com

- Affirmation Crafting Template
- Goal-Setting Workbook
- Visualization Journal

Daily Planner Template

- Morning: Affirmations, Visualization, and Gratitude
- Afternoon: High-Impact Actions
- Evening: Reflection and Gratitude
-

Recommended Reading

- *The Power of Your Subconscious Mind* by Joseph Murphy
- *Self-Mastery Through Conscious Autosuggestion* by Émile Coué
- *Think and Grow Rich* by Napoleon Hill
- *The Secret* by Rhonda Byrne
- *The Power of Now* by Eckhart Tolle

www.ingramcontent.com/pod-product-compliance
Lightning Source LLC
Chambersburg PA
CBHW060207070426
42447CB00035B/2782